The Farmers' Frier

The Farmers' Friend

•

Harry Shutkever

Elliott & Thompson
London

Contents

•

Author's Note

·

Cattle buyers come in all shapes, ranging from ultra-serious young bloods continuously worried about making the odd blunder, to the seasoned veterans, chain-smoking and unflappable. 'Survival of the fittest' is the only valid game-plan and a large dose of self-confidence or what's referred to nowadays as 'bottle' is called for. So after those lacking the vital ingredients in sufficient quantities have fallen by the wayside, what we have left is a crowd of hard-heads. This is not a complaint and while freely admitting that there were times when the fight was worth more than the prize, I have always enjoyed such company and have friendships that go back some forty years to prove it.

There was however, a most memorable villain that made an impression on me that lasts to this day. The most dangerous thing about him was his sense of humour – he could make you laugh even while picking your pocket. This joker, who hailed from the southern counties, introduced himself to me as, 'John, the farmers' friend' which was funny enough to be sure. But when I come to think of it farmers couldn't keep producing animals if there was no one prepared to buy them, so perhaps in varying degrees that's what we all were.

Prologue

·

Now don't get me wrong. My dad was solid gold, and I wouldn't have swapped with anyone, then or since. But he had somewhat unorthodox methods and ideas that could be a bit frightening. He scared me more than once when I was a lad, and quite often since, but he always acted for the best even if it didn't seem too clear at the time.

He never hit me; in fact he never hit anyone, because he had no need to. His icy stares, his cast-iron logic, and the way he had of putting his arguments across, were devastating enough on their own. When I asked my mother, a very gentle and cultured lady, just what it was that attracted her, she didn't have to think about it. 'However wrong he seemed to be, he always turned out right in the end.' This was a large part of the trouble. On those very rare occasions that he got it wrong, it was the devil's own job to convince him. The easy way out was to give in, which is what I usually did. There was also an inborn clash of personalities where this 'father and son' partnership was concerned because the natural, unadulterated Harry Shutkever takes after his mother. My dad realised very early on that if I was to succeed in a hairy trade like his, there were a lot of corners that needed to be rubbed off.

For the first twenty years I saw little of him, which formed a distance between us that took years to heal, and what contact we did have always had a negative edge to it. I was constantly being told what not to do: 'Don't climb trees; Don't play with fire' and such, and it was never because I might hurt myself, but rather because, 'I don't want any doctor's bills'. He was a hard man – rock hard – and if I have given any other impression I've failed already. But that didn't make him a bad father, and as he never said or did anything that might have speeded up the process, it was only as I evolved into adulthood that I began to realise it.

My three years in the British army started in Omagh, Co Tyrone, where I was suddenly catapulted into the care of the Inniskillins. I was taught to march, to shoot, to throw grenades and how to run for miles up and down Irish mountains, by a collection of corporals and sergeants who not only thought they were tough, but did their best to prove it. They would have been somewhat dismayed to be told, but compared to my old dad they were all pussy cats. My father's teaching methods would have been outlawed in the French Foreign Legion.

But I have survived… and this is the story.

Louis Shutkever – 1954

Apprentice Days

•

The low-pitched voice had been so grizzly and disjointed the night before that I'd rung off for several minutes without realising I'd understood neither the words nor their full implication – not got the message, in fact. I've done it before and no doubt I'll do it again although it really is daft. There I was, half-way through the following morning having already driven some fifteen miles through the rain with a probability of several more still to go and I didn't know the man's name, the name of the farm, where it was or what it looked like; only the district it was in and I could have been there already.

It's always the same, people who know their own landmarks take it for granted that everyone else knows them as well; especially the pubs.

'...Past the Crown and Anchor – left at the Swan – under the railway bridge and sharp right before you get to the White Lion.' (Before you get there mind, how are you supposed to know that?)

It was no use telling him I didn't understand (for the third time) because all he did was to shout louder down the mouthpiece, positively fatal was that, neither the machine nor my eardrum could make anything of it. So I did what I usually do, told him I knew exactly where he meant and that I'd be there at eleven o'clock tomorrow. Quite ridiculous of course, it was already half-past eleven and here I was, still cruising around those unknown country lanes like an idiot.

He'd rung to say he had a cow to sell and that somebody had recommended Louis Shutkever, so perhaps I should have handed the phone over and had done with it, although that would only have made matters worse. For one thing it was late, turned half-past ten, and once in bed my dad was a great sleeper. Also, for reasons that will be explained later, what I couldn't grasp over the phone was far beyond my dad. So I said I'd come, which was a very desperate thing to have done, because even when and if I managed to find the place, my troubles were merely beginning. Up till then I'd never bought a cow in my life.

Now if I'd been John Wayne my dad would have said, 'Go out there son and buy yourself a cow,' with much screwing up of eyes and patting of backs, and I'd probably have come back with half a dozen cows and a bandaged head as well. But I wasn't and he didn't. I missed the grand send-off mainly because it was Tuesday; my dad had already gone to Stratford Market, although it would have been little different had he still been there. I'd told him about the phone call over breakfast and all he said was to come on to Stratford afterwards and not be all bloody day about it. So all that was left was to sneak away like a thief in the night, which probably best describes the way I did it.

Looking back I now recognise it for what it was, my dad's special training technique. If there was a category in the *Guinness Book of Records* for pitchforkers his name would have been up there amongst the world's greatest. But at the time I didn't know, and the knowledge would have been cool comfort even if I had.

I am writing of April 1949 when I was twenty-one years of age and what I would call a 'second category' driver. I'd passed the phase where the journey to the village shop was high adventure but not yet reached the one where it is only a means of getting from one place to another. So despite the fact that I was late, lost and more than a bit worked up generally, I would have enjoyed the journey for its own sake, even in the rain. And if I keep mentioning that rain, it was because even for England in April it was no more normal than all the rest, the unknown destination, the unmet man, the unseen first cow, and the first time for everything. That rain wasn't a good honest English downpour that calls for a dash to cover or sou'westers and capes, it was a silent, sneaky, hazy affair, more in the Irish tradition, so that it was possible to overlook it and get soaked to the skin in next to no time. It didn't wet the windscreen but rather smudged it, the wipers then made a semi-circular smear on the smudge that was quite opaque and not enjoyable at all.

We come to the first miracle at about a quarter to twelve when I actually found the right place, which led straight to the second because I recognised it as such immediately. Both however did little to solve the main problem because a Bernard Miles-type rustic came forward to announce, 'the gaffer earn't 'ome', and it was only after some close questioning that I got him to confess to knowing the goings on in that neck-of-the-woods better than myself: "Es in pub 'avving 'is dinner'.

If the first two were minor set-backs, this latest bit was something of a disaster.

It is widely acclaimed that drinking and pubs play an intrinsic part in cattle buying and the meat trade in general, rest assured this is no fallacy; they did then and they do now. But that father of mine was unique in more than his training methods. He was a hard man, rock-hard, self-made in a tough trade that was going through tough times, a by-product of which was that he could swear at speed for a full ten minutes without repeating himself. Yet he hated pubs and didn't like drink. It was not a moral judgement and had nothing to do with ethics as such, although that is not saying he wasn't a clean-living man. He'd seen the calamitous end that various shaped bottles had brought to contemporaries and competitors so often in the past that he saw drink as a trap, along with flattery, unearned friendliness, and a good many other things that he avoided with great dexterity. He never lectured me about it; that was never his style, just the same the message had come through loud and clear. So much so that even now, some thirty years later and having survived three years of army life (the last one in the sergeant's mess), I am not a drinking man and know I never will be. Maturity of course is a great moderator, and these days I will go into a pub or a market canteen for a social half-pint and think nothing of it. But as I say, at the time, I was twenty-one and youth, as well as being tender, is also extremely intense, with black black and white white and nothing in between. So believe me, it was with some trepidation that I set out to find my first farmer from whom to buy my first cow in that absolute den of iniquity – a village pub. And all the time with my dad's teachings rattling about in my head and gobbling up adrenalin at an alarming rate.

Even seen through the drizzle it was a pretty little pub, small and squat with massive timbers encasing whitewashed squares, diamond-leaded windows and a crazy door, the sort of place the Americans have probably since discovered and taken back with them. A large, dopey labrador was sprawled just inside the doorway that I remember mainly because I tripped over him on my way into the gloom, and the first man I saw was the one I wanted. I knew it by instinct even before I'd asked the barman (or landlord) to point him out.

He was short and heavily built, something like the pub itself, with a thick neck overhanging a khaki cow-gown and a greasy cap perched on the back of his head, marking him out as a dairy farmer rather than the arable variety (they wear battered trilbies as a rule). His large face was both red and round, or at least would have been but for the half-loaf sandwich he was stuffing into it making those already small eyes almost disappear. He was my man all right. I knew it because he looked just like that grizzly voice I'd heard through the phone the night before. There were three other chaps with him and they were playing Shuv-ha'penny which, to the connoisseur, could constitute an unintentional clue to the district. To the best of my knowledge in most pubs the game is darts, but here we were in 'Shuv-ha'penny Land'.

He turned at my approach – just the head that is, the rest stayed where it was – and listened in silence to my introduction; not out of politeness or moroseness but because he had no choice – there was still something like a half pound of bread to be disposed of; mostly down his throat, the rest trickling down his front to join the liberal dusting already on the floor. When he did speak it was not to me, but turning the head a shade further he addressed the landlord (or barman), 'Get him a pint Bert, while I finish these silly buggers off.'

I didn't understand the first thing about Shuv-ha'penny and still don't, but it was obvious to me that they were good at it, my man probably the best. He didn't stop to size things up or take aim, just a quick tap with the palm of a thick, calloused hand and off shot his halfpenny, straight as a bullet, sometimes cannoning into others before coming to rest between the lines, just where he wanted it. That was the impression I got at least, his short nod and little wink to nobody in particular half suggested it and the lip-licking of his even more serious looking compatriots said the rest.

They were not the most talkative bunch, a few grunts and the odd profanity seemed about the limit, and although there was no money in sight there was also no doubting the fact that it was winning that mattered. Nothing for it but to watch from the sidelines and try to look as though I was enjoying that cold, tasteless pint that seemed as big as a bucket. How people can pour fourteen pints of the stuff down their throats in an evening I'll never know.

I would not have travelled seventeen miles to watch a Shuv-ha'penny marathon, not even world-class, and the hanging about was doing my state of mind no good at all. A few glances at my watch did draw a small concession but hardly what I had in mind. My man threw a knowing look at the nearest window and confided an opinion that '…it 'ud be blowing over just now…' which meant that either he was not the countryman he seemed or he was pulling my leg. That rain had settled in for the day and if I remember rightly went on all night and most of the day following.

However, suddenly it was over (the game I mean) and I never found out who won. I downed the remainder of the brew I'd been nursing, fast enough for most of it to go down my sleeve, followed him out to our respective vehicles and chased him back to his farm. And I do mean chased because, regardless of the fact that his old pick-up looked about ready for the scrapheap, he shot off round those lanes like Gonzallez's uncle. No sooner back in his yard he leaped out and made off toward the nearest gate, no time to close the van door, nor to look back and ascertain that I was in fact following; a marked difference to his whole attitude in the pub not twenty minutes ago. The Shuv-ha'penny player was back on his own muckheap.

We marched wordlessly abreast (I'd caught up with him by then) across two drizzle-soaked fields until, close to the far hedge, we came upon our quarry, a miserable looking heap that had once been a shorthorn cow. It could have been worse because she was sitting up rather than lying flat, and the head did turn at our approach, but the eyes were dull and uninterested, the spaniel-like ears were fully adroop, both ominous signs of deep trouble, and the stop-go breathing was like a badly worn sludge pump. I've seen some woe-begone sights since then but there weren't many to beat my first view of my first cow.

I'd been out with my dad many times and watched him buy cattle both at auction sales and privately on the farm so I should have known just what to do. I did know in fact. 'Never be in a hurry lad,' he'd told me a hundred times, 'keep them talking,' and not only did he advise me that way, he did it himself. He could talk – and listen – without any obvious effort, and never attempted to rush into a deal anymore than to hurry away after the current transaction was completed, but if he made it all look ridiculously easy it was because for him it was.

He was well-known and over the years had earned himself a reputation as a shrewd judge, so that when he put a value on an animal – or twenty or thirty for that matter – it was never really questioned even when not actually accepted. Furthermore the farmers he'd taken me to meet were old sparring partners with a wealth of interlocking reminiscences going back to the year dot. They were merely continuing one long conversation that had paused after the last deal, was reawakened with the present one, and would carry on at the next. Even after the old men retired (or died) the sons inherited it along with the farm and everything else, and although they'd heard it all before, they listened out of politeness and sometimes found out things they didn't know.

My case was vastly different. The rain-soaked pair who stood looking down at that roan bundle of misery were complete strangers, and my moon-faced Shuv-ha'penny player was being no help at all. He'd not so much as uttered a word since we left the pub.

'How long has she been lying there?' I'd decided to open the discussion from the technical end.

'She was up with the others last night when I phoned.' I'd discovered something already. Shuv-ha'penny was a practising fibber. Those piggy little eyes had not so much as blinked but he was having me on just the same. Even a novice like me could see that the poor old cow had not travelled more than a few feet in the last day or two. What a lousy start to a cattle-buying career.

'Will she load?' In layman's terms, my question simply sought to find out if she was capable of walking on to a cattle lorry.

'Course she will.'

Assertive as it sounded, I had strong doubts and waited to be convinced. He stepped forward full of confidence and brought a heavy flat hand down on her back. It sounded like a pistol shot and sent a spray of raindrops arcing away in all directions but that was all – the cow ignored him completely.

He then tried a different tack and shouted in her ear, with the same negative result, which didn't surprise me a bit. It's one of those techniques highly spoken of by older husbandmen but, to tell the truth, I've never known it to achieve anything. But then, with Shuv-ha'penny searching through his repertoire she took us both by surprise, and although she creaked a bit, she actually found her feet and even walked a few paces. Old Shuv-ha'penny never blinked an eyelid, but I knew he was as amazed as myself; nevertheless, it was good news all round. Once mobile, we were able to coax her back to the farm and install her in a loose box where she thankfully sank down on to some dry straw. Now all three of us could continue the negotiations out of the rain.

It was to take nearly an hour, and although I was determined to honour my dad's teachings by refusing to hurry, most of the delay was Shuv-ha'penny's own doing. He left me in no doubt that she was his best cow by repeating the information at least a dozen times, and all in a slow, lingering Shropshire drawl that made me feel like pushing him from one word to the next. I was taken for a conducted tour of his cow shed to see for myself the rosettes that had been won by his lesser animals, and thus reaffirmed my previous findings. I had not misjudged him. The faded condition of those ribbons said quite clearly that they'd been hanging there for years – before either of us was born. But then, he was a man in trouble and doing his best to salvage something from the wreck. Wouldn't I have done the same in similar circumstances?

By the time we returned to the loose box, I was beginning to think that perhaps he wasn't such a bad old cock after all when suddenly he spoiled everything by asking me £25 for his wretched cow and, what's worse, looking as though he meant it. There was not a hope in hell of his getting it. Of course; if I'd taken that thing back to my dad at £25 or anything like it he'd have disowned me (he always seemed on the point of it anyway). Just the same, it made the fiver I was on the verge of offering stick in my throat, so the next few minutes delay was all mine.

'Six quid,' I declared, after standing for a minute or two with head on one side in a massive show of concentration. 'I'll give you six quid and you can have it in notes.'

He stood there like a bull ready to charge and that was when I noticed his left eye was brown – like a lion's, and the other was grey – like a wild boar's. Without a word he stormed out of the building and as there wasn't a river handy, it occurred to me he might have been going for his twelve-bore (the cattle-buying business is not the easiest way of making a living). But he soon returned with nothing more dangerous than an armful of sweet smelling hay, which he dropped close to the cow's nose, after which we both stood in silence and watched her ignore it. That cow hadn't long left in this world, whether he sold her to me or not.

'Fifteen pounds,' he said, with his best cow looking away from both us and the hay. 'Got a bit of a chill that's all and I haven't got time to mess with her.' It was a massive slide in the right direction, but still no good whatsoever.

'Seven,' I said, 'I'll give you seven and that's the lot.'

The cow then proved to be as awkward as her owner. She choose that precise moment to start sniffing at the hay and Shuv-ha'penny's little eyes lit up like lanterns, but she didn't actually eat any and, after a bit, lost interest completely.

'I'll take a tenner lad, no less. The bloody knackerman would give me that.'

He was a hard man was Shuv-ha'penny, which is probably why I've never bothered to look him up since, but he had made a fatal mistake. A couple of weeks before she would have looked different altogether and I might have been glad to give him his twenty-five pounds for sausage meat. By now it was obvious that she was desperately sick, almost certainly tubercular, and the only thing left was dog-meat. Furthermore his threat to call in the knackerman was pure hot air. Even today when values have soared up out of sight, for a knackerman to give £10 for a cow that was 'down' she would need to be as big as an elephant (unless it was his brother-in-law). In those days they paid nothing, not even the hide money.

'If your knackerman has got a tenner for her you'd better get on to him, he's a better man than I am,' which was to be my final word – I'd decided to call it a day. Shuv-ha'penny also seemed to have given up – who knows, perhaps his brother-in-law was a knackerman. Then something happened that has recurred many times since. It didn't seem right to have come all that way and get a thorough soaking for nothing. It was admitting defeat. So, sitting in my car with the engine running, I wound the window down and stuck my head out.

'Another quid – eight pounds in notes if it's any good.'

Shuv-ha'penny had nearly reached the house. He turned back and came in close. 'I'll take nine.'

'The lorry's only down the road at Stratford Market. I'll shoot off and get it and if she'll walk on, I'll give you eight pounds-ten – and that's it.'

I stuck my right hand out into the rain, palm upwards, and he hit it, which is what cattle dealers call shaking hands. (He really did shake mine – for a moment or so I thought he'd broken it.) It's more a gesture of finality than friendship, closely akin to the auctioneer's hammer, and it's remarkable how effective so simple an act can be. I've bought hundreds of cattle in that way over the years, some from well-known villains and scoundrels, yet the number of deals that have come unstuck through back-sliding or welching after being thus finalised could be counted on one hand (are you listening, modern house-salesmen?).

I was back at Shuv-ha'penny's muckheap in less than half an hour, with the successful conclusion still in the lap of the gods. But my cow (and I say 'my' cow because since the handshake that's what she was) didn't let me down. The warm, dry atmosphere of the loose box must have revived her spirits because rather than just walk up the ramp into the lorry she skipped up like a spring lamb, surprising the both of us and delighting at least one. I gave Shuv-ha'penny his notes, counted out one by one into his large, grubby hand, and shot off back to Stratford to show my dad just what I'd done.

After I had dropped the ramp and opened up the side gates he did me the honour of climbing inside and listening to the purchase price, but that was all. He didn't touch her, hardly looked at her, and made no comment either by mouth or eye.

'You know Parker's place don't you?' he said, having walked down the ramp and reached dry land. 'There's two more there. Go and pick them up and take the lot in – and don't mess about, that bloody old thing'll snuff-it if you're not careful. Then come back here, there'll be a load to go home.' And that was it – business as usual. The welcoming committee matched the send-off.

Nothing.

We were never in the knacker-meat business ourselves and, in fact, at that time we had no slaughtering facilities of any description. But the

ability to handle 'knackers' or 'screws' as they were termed was important, far beyond the profit it earned, which is not saying that that was not
also vital.

A cattleman would not go very far without knowing the local farmers,
and how better to build up a connection than by spotting a lame, old, or
otherwise worn-out animal and offering to buy it. The knackermen
themselves made the job easy by paying little or nothing for them, so all
it needed was a few pounds in cash, a quick removal operation, and providing we weren't too greedy about it, we'd made a friend for life. And
what helped us to make friends also helped to keep them, so for many
reasons our knacker cow connections were the key to several doors.

We were agents for four separate dog-meat kings, and as useful to them
as they were to us. The problem for the knackerman was that although
they contracted to provide for regular outlets there were no places where
they could obtain constant supplies, so that, although as I say, they stole
the odd cow or two on the farms, there were times when they faced acute
shortage. The likes of Shutkever and Son, delivering direct to their dens
could come in very handy, despite the fact that my dad knew his cows to
the last dead-weight pound and there was not much chance of stealing
the usual margin from him. It was not big business by any means; a useful sideline would best describe it, yet this long established set-up,
admirable as it was, was to lead to our only serious clash with the law. But
that's another story.

I delivered the three cows, mine and the two from Parker's, to our tame
knackerman, then doubled back to the market for the rest of the day's
purchases, finally arriving back home by about six o'clock with the day
far from done. Home, by the way, was a fifty-acre farm some eight miles
south of the city of Birmingham – it is still my home and I'm sitting there
now.

The farm is not low-lying but it's flat, and in wet winters such as the
one slowly receding at the time, inclined to become waterlogged, so that
our cattle were still indoors, although the winter chores were beginning
to drag and the feedstuffs to vanish. So instead of simply opening the gate
and 'letting them go' the new arrivals had to be installed in our somewhat
antiquated sheds and loose boxes, fed and watered and tucked away for
the night. I was no longer alone however because there was a farmhand,
Jim Cook, another big influence who worked for us for twenty-six years
and left on a Thursday. (Strange that.)

From my earliest recollections right up to my army call-up, Jim Cook
was a very central figure. If my dad was not away at business or at the

greyhound track he was usually asleep on the sofa, so I suppose in a way, Jim Cook sort of brought me up. He was good fun at times, and on rare occasions would plonk me on his crossbar and take me home with him at dinner time. I can even remember sitting under his dinner table and being fed tomatoes by his rolly-polly mother. But he could also be a bit of a bully, and from a very early age he used to make me work. In fact it was Jim who taught me how to work, how to enjoy work, and how to take a pride in work. I had two brothers, one older and one younger, but they wouldn't stand for Jim's antics, so although we were always friends they seemed to go their way and I went Jim's way. All the work on our farm was done by Jim Cook, with myself an ever-willing helper. My dad was a top class cattleman, his sphere being all at the business end, but he was never a farmer and did no farm work of any sort. He didn't believe in manual labour at all in fact, and one of his perpetual grumbles about me was on that very topic. 'You'll never amount to anything lad because you waste too much time working.'

I know what he meant and admit he was right but it made no difference. I liked farm work and went right on doing it, which is just as well because he piled so much on there was really no choice.

Then there was Jim. He pulled just as hard, but in the opposite direction with me left hanging somewhere in the middle, busy as a bug in a bottle. It went on for years, and if I gave Jim a hand on that particular evening, it was more than for the love of it. My car was still stranded at Stratford Market and somebody was needed to come with me to retrieve it. Jim had taken a few cows to sell at Stratford that morning and should have brought my car back earlier, but my long haggle with Old Shuv-ha'penny had upset the system and he had come back as a passenger with the first load. Incidentally, I should say that in those days overtime had not been invented, and on the principal that what was done today was not left till tomorrow we worked until we finished. I don't think he really minded an evening trip to Stratford and back, but he would never have said so, because he was a bit like my dad was Jim Cook.

That memorable day finished at about nine o'clock, and although my dinner had long been cooped up in an old-fashioned black kitchen range (gone now like a lot of other things) there was not much the matter with it. One of the basic rules in the house of Shutkever was good food and plenty of it, and those who are expecting to be told that this was the result of my mother's culinary genius are in for a disappointment. My mother was a soft spoken, gentle lady of great rarity, the very best this

world has to offer, and if she features little in this story of the meat business it's only because she played no direct part in it. She had soft hands
and a lovely smile, and could converse easily and fluently in four lan-
guages, but for the moment I must sadly confess that she couldn't boil
water.

My dad was not a man to be stymied by so small a problem however,
and didn't let the fact that he was virtually penniless stop him from
procuring the services of a housekeeper-cook, a girl called Laura who
came to us in 1924 (three years before I was born). He discovered her on
his travels working as a kitchen skivvy for some old skinflint of a farmer
who considered she owed him so much for the attic she slept in and the
food she ate there was no need to pay her at all. My old dad soon put a
stop to that, and his judgement proved as right in that as it did in most
other things.

Laura could (and did) milk the cow, help in the fields, keep the house
clean and me scrubbed and presentable (whether I liked it or not) and
deal with any other household tragedy as it came along. She cooked like
an angel, and pandered to my somewhat finicky taste to the extent that
it took three years in the British Army to put things right. She stayed
with us until she died of cancer in her sixties some seven years ago.

After dinner we sat about listening to the radio and discussing this and
that, but although I was waiting for it my dad didn't mention my cow at
all and seemed to have forgotten about it completely. So just to fill in the
missing pieces I'll say here and now that she came to £15, a satisfactory
début that had little to do with my buying prowess or the cow's actual
value. Fifteen pounds just happened to be our knackerman's top price at
the time. Complications now arise.

What I say is, even without my cow my dad would have received no
more for Parker's two, if he'd stood on his head, and despite the fact that
they were bigger and better, this was true. But he saw it somewhat differ-
ently. No knackerman in his right mind would have handed out fifteen
pounds for an old banger like Shuv-ha'penny's best cow (not even to
Shutkever), which was also true.

Now this sort of conundrum might sound silly, irrelevant, and childish
even, and would have been but for one important consideration. Despite
the fact that I helped with the farmwork and neither received nor
expected anything for it, I didn't work for my dad and neither were we
partners. Our business activities, the cattle we bought and sold, were
entirely our own, which might sound a bit cockeyed in this day and age
and probably was even then, but it was my dad's way of doing things.

He'd always stood on his own two feet and it was his intention that I did likewise – but I'll be coming back to this later.

At about ten o'clock he got up to go to bed, but at the door he turned, held up four fingers and glared at me through them. 'He was lucky you went instead of me, that's what I'd have given him lad – four pounds and no bloody more – not a button.'

Take it from me – life with Father was never easy.

Wythwood Farm – c.1944

Genesis

·

My dad never spoke much about his early life and I've come to the conclusion that the process of surviving kept him so busy that he'd forgotten about it. What little I do know came from his brother, an old sick man who spoke no English whatsoever, and I had to travel half way round the world to find him. They were two of a family of five, the children of a village butcher in Russia (Smogon was the name he said although I can't find it on my map). That was as far as my long lost uncle could go because at sixteen my dad ran away from home, wriggled his way out of Russia bound for America, and they never met again. But of course I can do a bit better than that because for one thing I know he never got there. Lack of funds and the 14-18 war conspired to shorten his journey to the extent that the furthest west he ever got was looking at the Atlantic from Liverpool docks; a virtually penniless alien who spoke no English, had no job, and was a Jew as well – that's what I call starting from less than nothing. The few snippets I know of this period are not really part of this story so we move up some eight years by which time he was working as a kosher butcher in Birmingham, married and living above the shop.

Lewis and Lovestone, my dad's kosher butcher shop was a partnership, Lewis being an anglicized version of Louis, and Lovestone the name of his partner. Although I never met Harry Lovestone, I believe him to have been an easy-going and likeable man, with long family connections to Birmingham. His good looks and bright manner made him a real asset at the shop counter, but he had no knowledge of cattle and was not gifted with the business brain of his partner. This left all the serious side of the business firmly lodged in my dad's department. I don't know the actual situation at the time, but it appears that being an alien disqualified my dad from running a business, so joining up with Harry Lovestone, who was not only English-born but also an ex-serviceman, allowed the necessary licence to be issued. The partnership was in fact something of a shotgun wedding from the start.

Although not generally known, there are very strictly imposed Jewish Laws which leave a kosher butcher with a trading problem. Rabbinical thinking separates flesh from life and considers life as blood, so it is only permissible to eat meat that has had all the blood removed. To comply with this criteria, all the veins must be taken out, a highly skilled process called porging. But to porge hindquarters (without ruining them) was considered way beyond the capabilities of anyone over here, so consequently only the forequarters of any animal, beef or lamb could be considered kosher.

My dad capitalised on this trading problem by building up a connection with several local butchers and selling all his surplus hindquarters to them. The butchers liked his meat and were soon clamouring for more, so logically enough, it didn't take him long to realise that there was more money in this new venture, and certainly far less hassle. The result was that he gave his share of the shop to Harry Lovestone, tenanted a stall on the cheap side of Birmingham Market, and became a wholesale butcher. That was way back in 1927, the year he bought this farm and also the year I arrived.

My mother might have been Russian and might have been Lithuanian. She wasn't too sure herself because she came from Kaunas, a town perched right on the old border which, I'm told, fluctuated a few miles either way from time to time. It's immaterial really because the whole lot was gobbled up by the Soviets years ago, and I know she always thought of herself as being Russian. Like my dad she had never intended to stay here permanently and had only come originally to visit her married sister in Scotland.

Because she had a German name (Bach – like the composer), when the 14-18 war broke out she was refused an exit visa and became a sort of illegal immigrant in reverse. I've included this tiny reference to my parents' background to show just how lucky I have been. I am as English as the trees in my orchard and yet, but for a series of unconnected accidents, I might even now have been struggling in the financial and political mess on the wrong side of Churchill's Curtain.

By comparison my own early life was normal enough to be mundane. Shakespeare himself would have been hard put to make it sound much different to those 'what I did on my summer holiday' things we were made to write every year. One aspect however I will mention. It's no longer the beast it used to be but it has dogged me through the years and I know I'll never be able to shake it completely. It's this religion business I'm referring to, although the problems it caused were all of a practical or social nature and never really religious at all.

It started at an early age when, at a cost I now know he could ill afford, my dad employed a daily taxi to take me eight miles to the Jewish school in Birmingham. I have since tried to analyse my parents' motivations in this but without any real success. They were not deeply religious by any means and kept only the barest essentials of a Jewish home, but neither were they hypocrites in any shape or form. At best, I think the aim was that I should mix with Jewish people and absorb enough folklore to carry me through high-days and holidays without making an idiot of myself. If that was the case it has worked and I'm not ungrateful for it, although the cost in terms of misery was exorbitant. At worst (and with hindsight), it could be that secretly they thought that the old ghetto people from the kosher butchering days were expecting it to be impossible for a child to be brought up correctly, isolated by distance from the main herd and they were determined to prove them all wrong.

The kids at the school were just like any other kids (which could have been the first lesson) and I made friends there that I've kept to this day. But the background was so very different that Shutkever, the farmboy from the outback was considered something of a freak by children and teachers alike. I know this for a fact because, years later, whenever I came in contact with any of my old chums, they invariably opened the conversation with questions like 'Have you milked the cows?' or 'Have you fed the pigs?' or some such drivel, which always left me with the impression that they thought of me as a cross between Robinson Crusoe and Dr Dolittle.

Generally speaking the school itself was of a low academic standard, and basked in the glory of its brighter pupils, whose consistent high exam results could only have been the product of brain power one hundred per cent inherited. As for the Hebrew – that was crammed into a period of about three-quarters of an hour a day and so badly taught that I've forgotten most of it. But I hated that school mainly because it was in the city, and day after day I sat waiting for four o'clock so that I could be dashed off back to the farm to be trampled on by carthorses, yelled at by Jim Cook and generally become human again. So what I did on my summer holidays was live – and begrudge every minute of every hour that brought me nearer to the daily imprisonment without trial that constituted being 'correctly' brought up.

The rest can be said in a few short sentences. I always had a leaning towards things mechanical and my formal education finished with a two-year course at a technical school that I not only enjoyed but have found useful ever since. Then followed an apprenticeship to the television trade which was never completed. Factory life was not to my liking (the city again) and I was actually glad to be called up for military service at what turned out to be the tail-end of the war. The next three, khaki-clad years were busy and happy, showed me quite a bit of the world and probably taught me more than all the rest put together. I emerged from Aldershot demobilisation centre in April 1948, a fully trained vehicle mechanic, sun-tanned and fit, and clutching a cardboard box containing a grey striped demob suit that I never actually wore – I gave it to Jim Cook.

It sounds a bit strange now, but there was never any mention of my following my dad into the meat business, and thinking back I can only reach two possible conclusions. Either he had found the going so hard and demanding that he hoped I'd find something easier, in much the same way as I have never encouraged my own sons to follow me. Or, and by far the most probable, he thought I wasn't up to it. What's more, and at the risk of sounding completely daft, at that time and aged twenty-one, I didn't know precisely what my dad did for a living. I knew my father's time as a kosher butcher was over. All well and truly in his past. He worked now as a wholesale meat merchant in Birmingham market, though I never had any clear idea of how he spent his working hours. He was always vague, never really talking to me about what he actually did all day. He was up at the crack of dawn and gone long before I emerged, and by the time I came home he was usually asleep on the sofa. In fact that is how I best remember him through the early years, a figure lying on the sofa and not to be disturbed. Most of my time at home was spent out of doors doing my best to keep Jim Cook happy and not always succeeding.

All that came to an end most abruptly. One day I was working the farm with Jim and the next I was off to the cattle market with my dad, no discussion, no consultation, no decision – nothing! The Shutkever pitchfork came out and I was in.

The first thing I discovered was what a grand swearer my dad was. I know I've mentioned this before, but it really was amazing. Foul language in varying degrees is as common at cattle markets as it is in the army; it sort of grows on you, so perhaps that was where he picked it up. It came as something of a surprise just the same, a shock even, because I'd never heard him swear before. In fact, if in an unguarded moment I ever slipped out the odd naughty word, my dad would say, 'That's Jim Cook again… you should keep away from him.'

He'd learned his English at a night-school when he first arrived. In fact, it was the only school he ever attended because in Old Russia, education was only for those who could afford it. He could read quite well and could also write, although his letters were a bit shaky and he avoided writing whenever possible. His spoken English never became fluent, not so much because of an accent but rather through saying things the wrong way round, especially if he was annoyed or in any way put out. Over the telephone he had difficulty in making himself understood all his life. Yet when it came to oaths and profanities a most remarkable transformation occurred. When he swore his English was perfect. The next thing I learned was equally startling and also far more important. Louis Shutkever was no longer a wholesale butcher in the normal sense and neither was anybody else, because by that time and for some eight years past there was no such thing. From the beginning of the war until meat rationing ended in 1954, the whole industry was taken over and run by the Ministry of Food – a sort of temporary nationalisation so to speak – and along with all the others, my dad received a monthly cheque for the use of his business. If I remember rightly the actual sum amounted to seventeen pounds a month and as that was classed as unearned income, there was not a great deal of it left by the time the Inland Revenue had grabbed theirs. Fortunately there were other things.

The bowler-hatted brigades in London dreamed up a system to enable the Ministry of Food to handle and distribute the country's meat which, in theory at least, was scrupulously fair and British to the core. It is important that we understand the bare bones of the thing otherwise there's a very real danger that we will all get lost. The best thing, I think, is to set down the main theme now and deal with any further complications as they arrive.

The country was divided into areas each with their own killing and distributing centres, which were in fact the abattoirs and wholesale depots that had been taken over. These were supplied from collecting centres, normally cattle markets and still run by their respective auctioneers, some even serving a dual purpose being ordinary cattle markets for most of the week and Ministry of Food collecting centres for one appointed day. Tables of grades were worked out for all types of animal (cattle, sheep, pigs) and based on percentage of dead meat per live hundredweight, pound, or score and these grades represented the prices paid which were announced in advance on a sliding scale throughout the year. For example: If a bullock weighing ten hundredweight was graded 'A' and the current price for that grade was £6, the owner would receive £60 for the bullock. Sheep were paid for by the pound, and pigs by the score, but the principle was the same. At every collecting centre there were two graders, one to represent the butcher's interest and one acting for the farmer, and between them they arrived at the correct grades for each animal – all fair and British as I have said. Just to keep the party clean there were also head graders and super graders who periodically swooped down unannounced from hidden heights, to ensure there was no jiggery-pokery going on. I should also mention that if a farmer was not satisfied with the grades offered, he was quite free to withdraw his cattle and take them back home.

Well, that's the theory anyway.

The trouble was that there were serious flaws in the system and all stemming from the same root cause – graders were men and not machines, and men can, and do, make mistakes. Also it must be said, the really qualified, the top dogs on both sides of the industry, were too busy to take on such duties which were often left in the hands of lesser men, the semi-retired, the commercial failures, or worse than that, the busy-bodies, or worse still the money-hungry. Then, at great risk of offending my many farmer friends, I'll say that very few farmers know much about the meat content of the animals they spend their lives producing. They know about breeds and behaviour patterns, about diseases and cures, and many farmers are fair hands at judging live weights. When, however, it comes to meat and dead weights, it's a different story and understandably so. The butcher, on the other hand, takes over were they leave off and providing he's a real butcher, a man with his own slaughterhouse (as against one who buys lumps of meat without knowing much about where they come from) has the whip-hand every time. So what usually happened at the collecting centres was very much a one man show, the butcher-grader doing all the work while the farmer-grader walked about, feeling and poking and making all the right noises, and getting paid for his trouble as well.

I'm not saying that the system was a shambles or that it was constantly abused, it probably worked as well as could be expected. What I am saying is that it was not the unbiased, super-fair arrangement it was designed to be. And the door was open. I must emphasise that what I have written about farmer-graders v. butcher-graders cannot be applied to them all. There were thousands I never met and there must have been many exceptions, although I only knew of one. What I have said about the system however, I stand by to the letter.

The graders at Barnt Green, where my dad graded his cattle, were whiter than white, let's have no mistakes about that. At Barnt Green, the only arguments were between one grade and the next, small-money as they say, and never called for villainy of any sort. My dad needed a fair crack of the whip just the same, but he didn't need to corrupt anyone in order to get it. He relied instead on a subtle mixture of bluff and charm, and was exceptionally good at both – he wasn't a Russian for nothing. In any case the sort of villainy I was referring to called for special circumstances, special types of animal, and a certain type of villain, neither of which could be found at Barnt Green. It was when I started attending a different grading centre that the truth began to dawn. What is needed is the type of animal that can be converted from one category to another.

Bull calves that have been castrated badly or late can still retain bullish characteristics and appearance and are called stags. A 'staggy' bullock can be bought at bull price; £3 a hundredweight or there about, so at nine hundredweight such an animal would come to £27. However, if the buyer has a tame grader in his pocket, that same animal could be entered on the grader's form as a bullock and at bullock price; £6 a hundredweight, would come to £54. An even better and more common case would concern a certain type of cow.

Many cows, especially first time calvers, don't always manage to supply their offspring with milk in sufficient quantity and sometimes never at all. Their udders either don't develop, or shrink back almost to where they were. The buyer points out that the animal has in fact produced a calf, and makes such a fuss about it that the opposition is put off and he manages to buy her at cow price, about £3 a hundredweight. His tame grader then accepts her as a heifer and the Ministry hands out £6 a hundredweight – £60. These two examples are exaggerations. A young cow that closely resembles a heifer would cost more than a normal cow, but there would still be the sort of scope I have suggested. These are the most common areas for villainy in the old Ministry system, but we'll come across a couple more later.

All this I learned on a crash-course during the next few weeks as I travelled around the farms and cattle markets, seeing and hearing as much as I could and saying little as possible. I also learned how my dad earned his living – and nearly forgot to mention it. He bought cattle and sheep as before (never bothered with pigs in those days) but instead of killing them and selling the meat as a wholesaler should, presented them at various collecting centres three times a week. The animals were first weighed, the graders did their usual poking bit then offered a grade, which was accepted without blinking an eye, or refused after handing out a good cussing. It sounds simple but it wasn't (as should become evident in the following chapters). However, it was a living and the fact that we managed to survive the period and even make progress must prove something, although I'm not sure what.

So now to conclude what has been, in the main, a chapter of explanations, I will go back to that 'standing on my own feet' aspect I alluded to, and my dad's method of bringing it about. The system was unique, there's no room for doubt, because only a man like my dad could have dreamed it up and only a mug like me would have stood for it. He never gave or loaned me money, neither did he pay me wages. All the work I did on the farm, then and since, has been a labour of love. What money I had was almost entirely made up of army credits, and because I neither drank nor smoked and had risen to the dizzying rank of staff sergeant, I came out of the army worth £166. With that I bought a cattle lorry, taxed for the year and with two spare tyres, and when I say there was still £46 left, it should point out just what manner of vehicle it was – a rolling junkyard.

The Ford Motor Company could never have disowned it because it still had their name on the front, but whose hand devised the open-topped, wooden-sided contraption on its back, I'll never know. It bulged and swayed with no provocation whatsoever, and even after several modifications, to take a full load down a steep hill was to risk the back of the cab edging forward enough to trap my belly against the steering wheel. With that mechanized death-trap I then undertook the transportation of my dad's cattle wheresoever he commanded, for which he was to pay me at the standard rate. It was Shutkever pure and simple, cost him nothing, built up my capital, and provided someone to do the tearing about at the cattle markets while he was learning. It has since crossed my mind that if my old dad didn't manufacture at least half of the things I found myself doing especially for my benefit, he must have been a very busy chap before.

That system carried on for quite some time, until shortly after Shuv-ha'penny's cow in fact, when came a sudden and most unwelcome change. By then I was buying the odd beast or two (to cattlemen they are collectively called beasts), perhaps six or seven on a busy week, feeling my way as it's called, when my dad saw fit to stop paying his transport bills, although I carried on exactly as before, farmwork and everything. Every load was logged in my little book until it was filled from cover to cover, and I kept it close to hand for years. I even mentioned it once or twice, although it did no good whatever. Perhaps I should have been flattered because it might just possibly have been his way of saying my apprenticeship was over.

But I didn't know then and I don't know now.

The Graders

•

In the beginning there was only one grading day each week, which occurred every Wednesday, and the clearest recollection to remain about the first time I attended was how absurdly strange I felt. It was exactly like that cold morning three years earlier when I woke up on a hard bed in Amagh Barracks, County Tyrone and discovered I was a soldier. In many ways it was worse because there, at least, I was surrounded by dozens of other slightly bewildered young chaps all in the same plight, whereas here, everyone knew what he was about and was getting on with it, my dad included.

It is now quite obvious to me that not one of them had the slightest inkling of how daft I felt, standing there, son of an established trade personality – celebrity even – and I didn't even know into which pen to unload the cattle I had just delivered. All those years I had been helping Jim Cook, unloading the lorries as they arrived, growing and harvesting winter feedstuffs, mending fences, penning, loading and sorting three times a week, and waving the lorries off without a serious thought as to what happened next. I can only liken it to a worker in a factory, so busy drilling his holes in his bit of metal he never has time to investigate just what it is he's helping to create. Equally absurd, I was in a village not eight miles from home and I'd never been there before in my life – I had to ask the way. I'd heard my dad mention a few names and everyone seemed to know me well enough, yet apart from the lorry drivers I didn't know a single man in the place. I know I ought to have done, but I didn't, and it left me feeling about six inches tall and daft as a brush.

There was no driveway into Barnt Green Market. Entrance could only be gained by swinging sharp right across a narrow road, halfway round a blind bend and immediately climbing a short, steep earthen bank that was only reasonably level for about half of the year. The rest of the time it alternated between wet and slimy ruts and glassy frost. It was a tricky manoeuvre, both entering and leaving, calling for some quick thinking, rapid gear-changing, and more than a little luck. Legions of headlamps, wings, and radiators have come to grief, impaled on those cast-iron gateposts at Barnt Green Market, but apart from tapping one or the other a few hundred times I class myself as one of the survivors.

Up that bank and between those posts and you'd travelled a good hundred years back in time. The collection of wooden stockyards and buildings formed an L-shaped arrangement along two sides of a square, perhaps a half-acre in size. On the left hand side and separate from the rest were the lamb pens, and further along on the same side was the piggery, all in the open where they'd stood for generations. Between the pigs and sheep and towards the centre of the area was the lorry wash, a plain square of concrete – that didn't slope enough – with a drain hole at one end and an infuriating hose pipe that always leaked from a dozen different places. Even when turned full on, it produced little more than a dribble. To make anything resembling a jet it was necessary to squeeze the end flat between finger and thumb, immediately exciting the leaks to the point where a few gallons of cold water shot up the nearest trouser-leg. The centre quadrangle was grassed over and was used only as a car park.

Despite the gallons of tar and creosote lavished on it from time to time, the whole place was slowly rotting away, an antique without any slight semblance of charm. Just the same, my recollections of Barnt Green Market bring me only pleasure and I mourn its passing, so that even the pervading smell (a not unpleasant mixture of rotting wood, creosote and cow muck) is stored away in company of many happy memories. It has all gone now, gobbled up by the house builders. I often wonder if the occupants of those semi-detached's are ever disturbed by the ghosts of animals and men who used to assemble there every Wednesday.

The first man to approach was old Frank the yard-man, drover, and general factotum, a man with long, matted snow-white hair that carried on down each side to mingle with a matching beard. A grand old chap was Frank, helpful and obliging, yet I was always afraid to see him bustling about among the cattle in case he dropped down dead. As it happened I needn't have bothered because although he looked about ninety, he was a mere child of fifty-four.

I got off to a bad start. Frank opened the gate to the end pen and beckoned me to back up, but when I dropped the ramp and opened up the side-gates, I was greeted by a most horrifying sight. Two of the ten bullocks were lying on the floor. The rest had trampled on them and mucked them up, a shocking mess to start the day off. Incidentally, this is an occupational hazard that cattle-truck drivers must always guard against and can be the result of cornering too fast, braking too hard, overloading, sheer bad luck or a combination of everything. On long journeys animals can – and do– die in this manner. Luckily, in this case, no serious damage had been done and they got up and dashed off with the rest, but looked like drowned rats just the same. My dad's timing was always immaculate, and without turning my head I knew he had come ambling up and was glaring at my back, but if he said nothing it was because I never gave him the chance. I slammed the ramp up and made a run for it, mainly out of cowardice mingled with battered pride, but also for a very good, practical reason. Back at the ranch, Jim Cook was waiting with two more loads and all had to be delivered and penned by eleven o'clock.

Of the hundred or so cattle that made up the weekly collection at Barnt Green (it varied with the season), about eighty per cent belonged to cattle dealers like ourselves, the rest coming direct from the farms. Officially it should have been first come first served, but by general agreement a system of sorts had evolved. The farmers went first, because they'd usually got other things at home that couldn't always wait, then the dealers followed in any order that suited – quite gentlemanly really for the meat business. Also incidentally, although I shall concentrate perhaps entirely on the beef side of the industry, we did in fact do a considerable amount in the lamb department. Personally I had little to do with it, mainly because my lorry was not fitted out with the necessary decks. Sheep were given to the transport contractors. In any case although not without its complications, the sheep side is a fairly run-of-the-mill affair and all I can think to write about it is that it's bloody hard work.

So having unloaded the rest of the consignment (and without further mishap) the next step I discovered was the 'ticketing-up' operation. Frank walked among the cattle with a bucket of thick glue in one hand and a flat stick in the other, and proceeded to dab two lumps of glue on each animal, with me following up to plonk two matching numbered tickets on the glue. But even in so mundane an operation, Shutkever insisted it be done his way, and he walked in with us pointing out each animal in the rotation he thought right – there was nothing haphazard about it. Once that was done, and providing we weren't running late, there now came what I was to discover as the nearest thing to a dinner break on any Wednesday for the next six years – tea and buns in Mrs Banner's shed. It was there I met Sid Neasome, the auctioneer, who, despite my mucky cow-gown and sweaty, dishevelled appearance, came striding over to introduce himself in a most gentlemanly and civilised manner. This man, who was a direct descendant of Frank Neasome, founder of Neasome and White, auctioneers, deserves a paragraph or two to himself.

Right back in the old kosher-butchering days, my dad had been attending Barnt Green Market and buying cattle under Sid Neasome. In fact, I believe it to be the first auction he ever did attend. His needs in those days were small, a couple of bullocks and a dozen or so lambs would probably have kept Lewis and Lovestone busy for the whole week. But when he became a wholesaler the situation changed, and people began to think he was treading on their toes. The meat trade in general has never been famous for its welcome to outsiders, the normal ploy being to take turn and turn about, to keep topping the newcomer's bid, even if it cost money to do it.

One representative of a well-known Birmingham firm, however, decided to speed things up a bit by warning Sid Neasome that Shutkever was short of cash (which was true enough) and that his cheque could not be relied upon. Neasome's reaction was far from the expected. He took my dad to one side, told him what he'd heard and offered him two months free credit. A gesture such as that would be somewhat rare even today. In those days money was really tight and wholesale-butchers, some well-established, were going broke every week, making this friendly offer into something dangerous, fool-hardy even. Shutkever was a proud man and refused the offer (with thanks) then, to demonstrate his financial stability, paid for the following week's purchases from a canvas bag full of six-pences, drawn from the bank especially for the occasion.

When I met Sid Neasome he was a small, lean man in his early seventies, a slightly stooping figure in shabby tweeds and sporting the traditional old English gentleman's gold watch chain across the front of his waistcoat. The face was somewhat pinched and the high cheek bones a mottled red, suggesting that a drop of scotch, 'just to keep the cold out', would never go amiss. But the eyes were clear and direct, the smile was genuine and the handshake firm, and when he said, 'I'm pleased to meet you, Harry,' I knew he meant it. One of my problems throughout my life has been to live up to the expectations of many such grand old men, who obviously respected my father and were watching the progress of his son.

Tea-break over, it would soon be time for the serious business to commence, but first there was to be another delay. A code of honour had come into being that decreed it bad manners to watch another man's cattle being graded, perhaps to avoid inhibiting the graders, and possibly because it was nosey and extremely un-British. So until our first number was about to enter the weigh-scale we kept away. My dad introduced me to a few market characters and we passed the time talking. It was all very friendly, as well as being part of my training, but once again, I found the whole thing something of an embarrassment. All those good people quite naturally took it for granted that I knew the meat trade inside out, and believe me, I was green as grass. I didn't even understand the questions, much less the answers. When I followed my dad into the grading area they could have fired the cattle from a canon and I wouldn't have been surprised.

Sid Neasome and his clerk overlooked the scene from a raised cubby-hole on the far side. The scale, with our first beast standing on it, was to our right and above it, the large dial registering the weight. We stood on the outside of the grading area, a narrow post and railed confine about sixteen-feet by eight, and in that small arena stood three men; Ernie the ring-drover and the two graders.

The farmer-grader was a short, stiffly-built man in his fifties, economic in word and gesture, although given to holding his head to one side and spreading his fingers when considering a judgement. The large, heavy-jowled face held small, restless eyes and I discovered later that under the battered pork-pie hat was a completely bald head. When he did speak, it was in the quiet voice of a man who knew what he was about. His part-ner, apart from another bald head, was a different kettle of fish entirely. He was rarely still. When his feet and body weren't moving, his hands and eyebrows were, and if the other one was inclined to be taciturn he more than compensated for it. The comments came dribbling out almost constantly, some as whispered asides to his pal, others with a wide-eyed questioning look at my dad. He thought himself the king of repartee but I'm afraid he was mistaken. Incidentally the graders at Barnt Green were the exception I mentioned earlier, here it was the farmer who was king and the butcher, the dupe.

The four of us nodded to each other. Ernie stepped across to open the scale door and old Frank prodded the first beast into the ring from behind, closed the front door and coaxed the second one in to take its place. I stood by my dad, with book and pencil to hand as instructed, and had already written in the first weight and ticket number, and we were off. The graders looked the animal over from each end, then changed places and repeated the process in reverse. Next, they felt it on the shoul-der, on the rump, pulled at the flank, felt the cod, perhaps a couple of times each. Then they went into a huddle, followed by another feel and huddle. Finally they nodded to each other and with the butcher-grader nodding his agreement, the farmer-grader looked across at my dad and said: 'A minus.'

'Not bloody likely!' said my dad, glaring and pointing to the far gate with his stick. 'Open the gate lad – that one goes home.'

The next was offered 'B minus' and the one after that 'Plain A', but the answer in both cases was the same –

'Back home!'

This is a rum business, I thought. I'd gone on booking the weights and ticket numbers, but I didn't know why. With the fourth, however, came a change. After the charade was over the graders offered 'B plus', and this time, after glaring at the animal for a bit, my dad gave a short nod and said, 'It's yours.'

Ernie then produced a pair of scissors and cut two long lines in the hair on the right side of the rump with a short line above, which was the Ministry's mark for 'B plus'. Eventually all our cattle had been through the weighing, prodding and poking routine, with three or four more finishing up in the 'back home' pen; the rest, scissor-marked and mingled with those already belonging to the Ministry of Food, and waiting to be transported out. On two occasions, the graders had given way and offered an extra point to their first decision. Then my dad confused me still further by pointing out four of the remaining seven and telling Ernie to 'mark 'em up'.

By then I was in a most unholy mess. I'd managed to get all the weights and ticket numbers mixed up and hadn't booked down the grades at all. I put it right later by copying it all direct from the clerk's sheet, thereby abruptly nullifying the whole exercise. My book was supposed to be a check to ensure the clerk had got it right. It didn't help me very much. My dad knew all about it because he'd peeped over my shoulder. He didn't say anything, just walked away shaking his head. The clear implication being, we'd all be better off if I'd stayed in the army.

The day was still a long way from done because there was still the lorry to be scrubbed. Twenty-six large animals had done their best to plaster it up and it had stood gently baking in the sun for the last hour or so. Believe me, it's rum stuff is cow muck. No laughing matter at all. In some parts of the world, I understand, they make houses out of it. But eventually it was done. I backed up and Frank helped me to load the three remaining 'back homers' and I was on my way.

Now here's a strange thing.

When, later that same day, my dad (who'd never been to school remember) went through the items in my book, he told me to the nearest ten shillings what each beast was coming to, knew what they cost, and how much they were earning, and he wasn't guessing – he knew.

Lichfield

•

My entrance to the world of cattle markets proper, as against Ministry of Food collecting centres, was made on a Monday in the neighbouring town of Lichfield. Again, incredible as it may seem, I'd never set foot in a cattle market before in my life. Much bigger than Barnt Green, the place absolutely buzzed with activity, making it necessary to keep close to the fence rails to avoid being run over by bunches of cattle being pushed towards the pens by stick-waving, oath-shouting drovers. The scale was different but my situation was the same. From all directions came nods of greeting for my dad, short stops in our preliminary tour of inspection, conversations, some with handshakes, others without, and shouted cat-calls which were exchanged on the move. These, as it turned out, were running jokes that went on for years, but at the time it was all a foreign language. I might just have landed on Mars.

There was also a predominance of nick-names. There was Smiler, for instance, whose permanent leer was the unfortunate result of a bone mal-formation and anything but pleasant. There was Wagger and Noddy and dozens more besides. In fact, there are men I've known all my life without the slightest notion of what their real names sound like. It took me until then to discover that my dad's name was Jake, although it only seemed to apply in that town and surrounding districts. Such honorary titles usually stemmed from things physical, but this was not necessarily always the case. To a few of the older inhabitants of our Thursday market, for instance, Jake was still known as 'Thirty-Bob', which dated back to the very early days when that was his top limit. The strangest of all was 'Kelly', and that wasn't at cattle markets at all but rather at the dog track (my dad's only deviation). I never had that one explained, but rather suspect it to have a religious significance and a distant derivation of 'the Cohen's and the Kelly's'. Far from being derogatory, such nick-names were a mark of fame. The fact I never earned myself one is not without significance.

Jake and I continued our tour until one o'clock, when the ringing of the bell summoned us to join the fast-gathering assembly in the cattle ring, and I say in the ring because that was where we went. In modern times cattle buyers stand, and even sit, in amphitheatre-type constructions around the perimeter of the cattle rings, heated in winter and sometimes even provided with vending machines. It's all become dull and civilised. In those days it was quite common for the whole thing to take place in the open – rain, snow, and everything, and standing in amongst the animals being sold.

Comfort is not everything and, strange to say, there were points for, as well as against. Farm animals are vaguely classed as domestic and compared with the inmates of forests and zoos, they most certainly are. But away from their own farms and surrounded by unfamiliar bustle and smells they usually range somewhere between the highly excitable and the downright dangerous. The inside of a cattle ring then was not always the safest place in which to spend long hours of the normal working life. On the other hand, it must be pointed out, we should not lose sight of the reason we were in Lichfield in the first place. Namely, to make money. Cattle buyers thrive on confusion, and in amongst the ducking and diving to avoid getting maimed, there was always the possibility of sneaking in the crafty bid without anyone realising from where it came.

There were no weighing machines at cattle markets. The animals came into the ring one at a time and were sold at so much each, the bidding being in pounds and shillings. It was up to the buyer to decide the weight, the quality, and how much he was prepared to pay. A sharp eye had to be kept open for defects, lumps and bumps, signs of disease, blind eyes (because not only are such animals awkward to handle, they can blunder through hedges and fences doing more damage than they're worth). The pitfalls are too numerous to mention. Time was also at a premium because cattle buyers are not the only ones who thrive on confusion. Auctioneers rattle on at a most alarming speed. Now, what I said in an earlier chapter about the tear and bustle that fell to me at cattle markets was all very true and not long a-coming, but for that day, and the next week or two it was mainly a watching brief. Little else was there to do but book down the cattle as my dad bought them, load them on the lorry and take them home (and learn).

Lichfield was never a favourite market of mine and in fact I grew to detest it. The auctioneer was a nice chap. Brisk and businesslike and stood for no nonsense, but he was fair and honest and there were a good many in his profession that were neither. Many of the farmers were among my dad's oldest friends and the selection of cattle was at least as good as anywhere else, so it would seem somewhat unprofessional to think in terms of favourite markets. Nevertheless, we all had them – including my dad. Stratford, the Tuesday market, was the one he liked best. For myself I can give reasons for preference and otherwise, and although they might seem trivial and irrelevant, I will set down a few and leave the reader to judge.

In the case of Lichfield the first thing was the timing. It started late and finished late, which left little time before to settle down to any serious farmwork and always led into a mad dash to get finished at night. Then there was the floor of the place, all blue bricks, slippery as glass in winter and a menace to animals and man. Those bricks were not cemented together and the cracks between filled up with a mixture of muck and water, so should it be necessary to enter a pen to sort out cattle, the bricks would rock about and squelch that unholy cocktail all over anything less than ten-feet high. Don't get me wrong, I was never afraid of a bit of cow muck but, faced with a long drive home, it didn't add to the enjoyment. But I think the real reason I disliked it was its locality, on the wrong side of Birmingham, making about two-thirds of the twenty-five mile journey meander through dull and uninteresting city streets, and as I've already said, I only come to life in the country.

Just the same, it was at Lichfield that things started to hum, but before I can describe how it came about I must explain why, and in order to do this I must delve a little deeper into the Ministry of Food's system. I will be brief to the point of brutality.

Bullocks and heifers were known as 'clean cattle' and for meat purposes were classed as top quality and paid for accordingly – and still are. Cows and bulls were lower grades altogether, and classed in the main for sausage meat and such. But in between there was another category, a female animal that had bred a calf but was not a cow – it was a cow-heifer. The two important points to remember are first, that a cow-heifer was worth something like £1.50 per hundredweight more than a normal cow and second, how to tell the difference.

A calf is born with a full set of teeth, eight in all, but as with humans they are milk teeth. At about eighteen months the middle two come out and are replaced by permanent teeth (called broad teeth) after which, at about six-monthly intervals the rest follow suit in pairs, until all eight are of the permanent variety and the animal becomes a 'full mouthed cow'. But as long as there still remained one calf tooth it was a cow-heifer. The problem for the cattle buyer was that unless he had looked into the animal's mouth there was no way of knowing; with that precious baby tooth she was worth perhaps £45, without it £30 – poles apart as they say.

Now it so happened that among the buyers at Lichfield was a dealer I shall call George. I haven't seen him for years but if it's true what they say about only the good dying young you can bet your boots he's still around somewhere. A very nasty piece of work was George, he didn't like me or my dad and didn't care much who knew about it. By now he would be about retiring age, but then he was in his prime, strong, active and not above resorting to violence even before everything else had failed. As there would be little gain in changing his name, then describing him in detail, there's not much else I can say. Personally I always found him ugly enough but then I'm prejudiced. In all fairness there might have been a certain outdoor ruggedness that some women – complicated creatures – might have found attractive, and if I didn't think so it wouldn't have bothered George too much, because I'm sure he did.

Another misconception of George's was that he thought Lichfield Market belonged to him, and anyone who dared go there to do business was trespassing on his property. He'd developed a technique regarding cow-heifers that was particularly suited to his natural talents. When a youngish-looking cow came into the ring he would make a lunge at it, hook his curved walking stick under its snout with his right hand, plunge a strong left hand thumb and index finger into each nostril, have a quick look into the mouth, then let it go. He was then in possession of privileged information, and it would not have been easy to try the same trick, because after one dose of such treatment animals will not readily stand for another. How he then used this violently attained privilege would depend on the circumstances, because the situation was more complicated than it might so far appear. It was always a possibility that the cow he had just mauled actually belonged to him, so that what seemed a crafty attempt to buy might have been an even more crafty attempt to sell. This incidentally was by no means unique to George, one way or another we all did it from time to time. So now he could do one of two things, either walk away appearing to lose interest then sneak in a crafty bid while no one was looking, or start waving bids about in an excited manner giving the impression he'd struck oil when, in truth, he was hoping to drop a cow-heifer on to Jake that wasn't a cow-heifer at all. And make no mistake, friend George was no fool – the stage lost a good man when he took up with cattle dealing.

I watched this pantomime for three weeks before deciding to do something about it, but said nothing to my dad, just in case I made a mess of it. The following week I arrived a little earlier than usual and this time, equipped with a pair of wellies, overalls and a hooked stick like George's.

I worked my way through every pen, from one end of the saleyard to the other, and any cow that looked even remotely young enough was

grabbed in the aforesaid manner and forced to submit to a dental exam-
ination. The bricks squelched and the muck flew and by the time I finished I'd been trodden on, crushed against fences, and cracked my dad's
best walking stick. But stowed away deep in my pocket was a scruffy bit
of paper on which was written every number of every cow that had
calves' teeth, and also one or two young-looking ones that hadn't, just to
be on the safe side. That father of mine was a real hard case. He looked
a bit cockeyed at the mess I was in when I found him shortly before the
bell, but he took my bit of paper without a word, read it, fully understood
it, and all he did was wink at me once before making his way into the
ring. But he did something else. He accepted my list of numbers without
question, acted on it as though he'd seen it for himself, and from my dear
old dad, that was compliment indeed.

Poor old George. He started performing right from the off and today's
cows hadn't forgotten the mauling I'd just given them. I'll give him his
due, he caught most of them, and hung on for his life, although they
dragged him about all over the place. Knowing what I did, his antics were
even more to be admired but, needless to say, they did him no good whatever. I caught my dad's eye once or twice but although he'd used up all
his winks and didn't so much as smile, I knew he was enjoying himself.

What a day that turned out to be. All George's traps and schemes were
avoided and he didn't know how, and he couldn't have taken a better
mauling than if he'd set about Mohammed Ali himself. There was more
yet. Somehow or other, we managed to make off with two cow-heifers
that neither George nor anyone else knew anything about. Of course, I'd
let myself in for a monstrous chore that was to keep me sweating for the
next six years.

Lichfield was a sizeable market and Stratford about the same, but our
Thursday market was bigger than both of them put together. In the busy
autumn season I was to claw my way through the horns and cow muck of
the Thursday market for an hour and a half every week, and I've got the
scars to prove it. Furthermore, the situation was to deteriorate as the
weeks went by because there were George's at every market, some friendly,
others not. It didn't take them long to see what I was up to, indeed some
of them were already at it. Before very long there was an army of us
beavering our way through the pens, so the chances of hitting the jack-
pot got slimmer by the week. Just the same, it had to be done, if only to
ensure we knew at least as much as the rest, and in any case, after that
first glorious day my dad took it for granted and held his hand out for my
bit of paper quite automatically – I never even got another wink.

With or without all the George's, those cow-heifers were always something of a tricky proposition because, even when you thought yourself home and dry, it was still possible to lose. Just imagine, I work my way through the squelch of Lichfield Market and standing there among the cows is a strapping great animal that looks as old as Methuselah's auntie. On an impulse, I decide to grab her and would you believe – she's got a calf tooth. On my list she goes. Trusting, as he is, my dad is seen to hesitate and cast a glance in my direction, but I give him the nod and he buys her. No-one says a word and after the sale I insist on catching her again to show my dad how clever I am. We go home in great spirits. On top of a normal day's business, we've copped an easy tenner. The following Wednesday, we take her with the rest to Barnt Green Collecting Centre. The graders do their usual poking act, then Ernie does a quick nose-grab, and the two bald heads go in close for a dental survey. And, lo-and-behold, the bloody little thing has gone and taken our tenner with it.

I couldn't invent so sad a story as that. Believe me, it happened many times, in spite of the fact that we took every precaution against it. Such animals were never kept an hour longer than necessary, and during that time only the very softest of grass or hay was let anywhere near them. My dad would have fed them on jelly and blancmange if he could have got them to eat it. It's funny when you come to think of it, who would believe that thirty-years ago a calf tooth weighing less than an ounce could be worth more than a quarter of beef?

Yet there were those who thought of nothing else. Cow-heifers at cow price were by no means easily come by, and not everybody was prepared to wade through oceans of muck to do it. So logically enough, it occurred to the more reckless that if they started with a full-mouthed cow, knocked the two outside teeth out and replaced them with sheep's teeth, they could manufacture their own cow-heifers and make a mint. All I can say about such dental deviousness was that it was an awfully serious way of making money – because large amounts of lumpy porridge awaited those who got caught.

I cannot leave this section on Lichfield Market without including the Ken Hammond incident. In an earlier chapter I referred to the very central part that drinking and pubs played in the meat business, and here we have an example that's just too good to leave out.

There were two Hammonds who regularly attended Lichfield Market, a father and son, busy men both. A television producer needing a sample of the old-time cattle dealers should have looked no further. The father was a gruff, hard-headed man; cloth cap, a bushy moustache in the 'Old

Albert' tradition and a fiery temperament to go with it. Son Ken was a dashing young blood, always larking about, laughing and likeable, but keen in business for all that.

I think they hailed from Derbyshire or perhaps a little further North, which would have accounted for their Yorkshire-type dialect, and also their love of the brew, for which both were equally famous. Hammond incidentally, was their real name and for two reasons I have decided to leave it unchanged. First, because I know that any surviving relatives would be sure to find the incident as comical as we all did, and second, because I couldn't think of another name that suited them better.

It was early in December 1950, or thereabouts, and there was something like six-inches of slushy snow lying about. Being in the busy pre-Christmas time of year, the ring was crammed with both cattle and buyers, all wallowing about in the slush. Ken Hammond was leaning against the railing and bidding for an animal, but bit-by-bit he started to lean further and further, until he keeled right over and finished up lying flat out in the snow. That would have been funny enough in itself, but it got funnier, because not only was he still waving his bids at the auctioneer, but his bids were being accepted until he actually bought the animal. Without attempting to get back on his feet he then looked up at my dad, who was standing close by, and said, 'If you don't buy 'owt you've got now't to sell, have you Jake?'

Jim Cook

With the Shutkever sons – Ralph (on right);
Sidney (in centre); Harry (on left)

Stepping Out

•

I once knew a man who liked to sing popular arias from grand opera. He certainly had the lungs for it and would have become famous except that he had a voice like a fog-horn and was also tone-deaf. This cut off his career at the roots as it were, but rather than stop him singing it merely forced it into hiding, the safest refuge being whilst driving along in his car. At such times he would really let it go. *Madame Butterfly*, *La Traviata*, *La Boheme*, he knew them all. But what he didn't know was that in the summer and with the windows down, his secret was scattered all over the parish. He was a quiet, serious-minded man and inclined to be somewhat introverted, so it could have been kindness that stopped anyone telling him. In any event it was harmless enough and not unproductive in its way – with lanes as narrow and twisty as ours, and him not the best of drivers, it was a good way of preventing accidents.

After several months travelling the cattle markets with my dad, all feelings of strangeness had long disappeared. I'd even reached the stage of passing opinions, pointing out animals that had seemed cheap and wondering why he hadn't bought them. This always drew a storm of reasons, often heated, laced together with profanities and accompanied by head-shaking to a degree that made me realise just what perfect sanctuary can be had by remaining silent. Just the same, although I might not have realised it at the time, I was sliding into the same situation as the phantom opera singer. I was mentally ready to chance my arm but with my dad breathing down my neck it was impossible. Many a time I stood staring at an animal waiting to come into the ring, weighed it up and even had an opening bid already formed inside my head. I actually got as far as sucking in a deep breath in preparation for shouting it out, but that was as far as it went. It would have stayed that way, I know it would, because apart from one remarkable exception that doesn't really count, I have never managed to buy an animal of any description with my dad looking on.

Although I find it difficult to imagine, even my dad was once a novice himself and not only was he aware of this mental predicament but, as always, knew and administered the cure. For reasons never forthcoming he decided to hide behind an excuse for once, but the truth of the matter is that his remedy was nothing new whatever – he brought out that pitchfork again. This was about the middle of July 1949, I remember the month because we'd just finished haymaking.

'We're a bit short of cattle for next week, you'd better slip down to Gloucester and get a load.'

That was exactly as he put it, and because it sounds a bit lame I'd better decipher it. First of all there's the term 'slip down' which was a great favourite with my dad. He'd never have said, 'I want you to put a fence up,' but rather, 'slip a bit of wire up there lad,' even when it actually constituted a long week's work. In this particular case his 'slip down to Gloucester,' meant a fifty-odd mile journey and, what's more, he told me on a Friday. Gloucester was on the Saturday, which only goes to show just how brutal he could be with that pitchfork of his.

Being 'short of cattle' meant more or less what it said, but was also something of a trade cliché, much used by everybody in those days. This was because the Ministry's scheme was designed for farmers' use and one of the rules stated that, in order to simplify transport and allocation arrangements, cattle must be entered for grading a week in advance. For the farmers this was no problem. They knew their own cattle and it usually takes them at least a week to make their minds up to sell in any case. With the likes of us it was a different matter entirely. Having said how many cattle we'd got we then had to go out and buy them. This resulted in a gigantic game of 'think of a number' which we played every week and although we got used to it, and it usually worked out, there were times of unforeseen shortages when we found ourselves genuinely 'short of cattle'. In the main however it was used as an excuse. If we knew of a farmer who had some fat cattle there was no harm in dropping in and making him an offer because we were 'short of cattle'. Or again, if a bid had been made and refused, it could always be increased by a pound or two for the same reason.

I can't say whether we actually were short on that particular week. I left all the serious stuff to my dad, but it didn't matter really one way or the other. He told me to go to Gloucester and that was all I was waiting for, although to be sure, I didn't sleep too well that night.

Gloucester was the exact opposite of Lichfield and at least twice as big. The journey was all along good, fast roads that ran through fine, open country and the place itself, although in the town, was spacious enough to avoid the claustrophobic atmosphere of the Monday market. It was all in the open; pens, ring, everything, and apart from the perimeter walls the only brick building I can remember was the auctioneer's office. The canteen was a wooden shed which was tucked into a corner and always looked to me as though it had just blown in from a cricket pitch, and the other thing I remember (which as far as I know was unique to Gloucester Market) was its collection of trees. They weren't saplings or overgrown shrubs but full grown trees, beeches and limes, I think; perhaps half a dozen or so, and scattered about the market itself, in among the cattle pens. For all its size there was a quaintness about the place, something like the old country fair that always reminded me of Barnt Green; even the smell was the same. I was keyed up and nervous and wondering what I'd let myself in for, but I liked Gloucester from the start although, to be sure, it set me a puzzle right away.

Gloucester turned out to be two markets in one; two separate and independent firms of auctioneers each with its own blocks of pens and its own sale ring, and all going on at the same time. So before I could decide which cattle to buy and how much to pay for them, I first had to work out which auction I was going to do it in. I still don't know why I picked the one I did (it was nearer to the canteen, mind) but even though I was to try the other one on several occasions I never could settle there and always returned to the first. After a tour of inspection that took me up and down the alleys, and which I now admit was more than a little procrastinatory, I pushed my way into the ring trying to look as though I belonged there but, believe me, it wasn't easy. With all its trees and old world quaintness, on that day and at that time Gloucester Market was very much Indian Territory.

I was in for a surprise that was to have far-reaching consequences, so although I'll set down what happened now, the rest will be dealt with as and when it unravelled.

'Old Jake's decided to let you out then.'

The statement (or question, the tone could have implied either) took me unawares because it came booming into my ear from behind and to my right. I turned to find a large man in a khaki cow-gown I instantly recognised as Harry Wooton. Not only did he hail from our district, Harry Wooton was a business acquaintance of my dad, and something of a local character.

'He doesn't know I'm here,' I replied, which we both knew was purest nonsense and just the first thing that came into my head. Harry then caught hold of my sleeve and turned to his nearest neighbour, a hatchet-faced, slightly built man in a khaki cow-gown and dark brown trilby.

'Do you know who this is Frank? It's Harry Shutkever, Old Jake's lad – just come out of the army.'

'Just', by the way, was about eighteen-months, but in countryman's terms that's nothing. Frank reached out and we shook hands, which seemed to me a bit formal in the circumstances.

'Met Jake once,' he said, in a slightly northern accent. 'You're bigger than him – must take after your ma.'

Trivial as it was, Frank's comment was true. My dad was not over-tall and I do resemble my mother. It also demonstrates a characteristic prevalent in the meat trade and countrymen in general; they notice physical details and remember them for years. By now several more had joined our gathering and Harry made the introductions in turn although, at the time, I was too confused to benefit much from it. Meanwhile, cattle had been entering and leaving the ring and the auctioneer's single-toned voice went rattling on in the background with no-one, it seemed, taking any notice. For the moment at least, Jake's Lad was the centre of attraction. I wasn't so much flattered by it as warmed, believe me it did me good, and Harry Wooton hadn't finished.

'Have you spoke to the gaffer yet?'

'I've only just landed.' Which was exactly how I felt.

Still holding on to my sleeve, he walked me over to the auctioneer's cabin, which put me in mind of a miniaturised railway carriage and was so high we both had to crane our necks to see who we were looking at. The auctioneer, who had only that moment crashed his hammer down to finalise the latest transaction, leaned forward to make our task that much easier.

'This here is Harry Shutkever and you'd better look after him. Don't worry about his cheque. If he doesn't pay you I will.'

The man above looked straight at me and gave a short nod. 'You bid up lad and I'll do the rest.' His was a southern drawl. 'A bit of new blood is just what we need down yere.'

To tell the truth I didn't much like the look of that auctioneer. On top was a narrow-brimmed derby (like the old-type bookie) and directly beneath, a pair of small, pale blue eyes that were both restless and bloodshot. The full face was a terrible mixture of deep red and blue, and if Sid Neasome looked as though he took the occasional nip, this one could quite easily have been living on the stuff. All I could see below that was a narrow-lapelled, brown-striped suit and a small hand that protruded beyond a four-inch expanse of white shirt-cuff to brandish the neat wooden hammer. The bookie image was further emphasised by the gold cuff-links and matching tie-pin, which were miniature horse shoes interlaced with riding crops. If the bookie image was the stronger there was also a hint of the confidence trickster, as well as a touch of old-time music hall, and I never saw him dressed other than I have just described.

As I later learned, Critch Pope, away from the auctioneering bench, was a polite, soft-spoken man of few words. I think there were connections with the racing world although I couldn't say for sure. Whether or not Harry Wooton's introductory comments had any bearing I couldn't say, but he seemed always on the lookout and I rarely had difficulty in registering my bid, however craftily I chose to do it. Like all others in his profession he could pause and linger in a most aggravating way before bringing that little hammer down, but he treated me, right from the start, no different to anyone else, which is what I best liked about him. He had no favourites, which should apply to auctioneers in general but unfortunately does not.

For the next hour or so I stood among the rest and watched the proceedings in a nervous silence. Every animal was scrutinised most carefully and in my mind I worked out how much they were worth then waited to see how near I had been. (I still go through this exercise although I now get much closer and it doesn't take half so long). But I made no bid. I only had to come near to bidding for the blood to rush to my head with such paralysing effect that I was rendered immobile, until either the price had gone too high or the hammer had come down. Perhaps it would have been better without Harry Wooton because then I would truly have been alone. As it was, through him and his associations, the spectre of Louis Shutkever was still hovering near, almost as though he was there himself.

But this could not be tolerated; a hundred-mile round trip and a day's time must not be allowed to fritter away gawping at other people buying cattle, and besides, Jake was not the only Shutkever with a bit of pride. Then, shortly before midday, she came unsuspectingly into my life; a neat, full-meated black heifer, plenty of hindquarter meat, a small head, and in short a perfect 'Shutkever-type' animal. My brain was hammering out messages like a two-stroke motorbike – she must be eight hundredweight – she must be grade A – and grade A being £6 per hundredweight, she must be worth £48, by which time the auctioneer was in full cajole.

'Come on lads, we haven't got all day, how much?'

'Thirty pounds,' I yelled, loud enough to rattle the leaves on the nearest tree, 'Thirty pounds.'

'Thank you for a quick start,' said the man above with another of those quick little nods of his. 'Thirty pounds – thirty – thirty – thirty, come on, let's get on.' I don't know if you've ever seen a radiator boil over, but I have, and that's just how I felt. I kept both eyes glued to that heifer so I'd no idea where the bids were coming from, but through the mists I heard the auctioneer saying, 'Thirty-nine.' So I said, 'Forty.'

'What's the matter with you all?' came the professional question from on high, '£40 for all that beef? Send for the police – there's a robbery going on here.' (What he actually said was 'yere's a robbry yere' – a pet phrase of his.) Somebody must have believed him because although much more slowly, the bids crept on. At forty-three pounds, fifteen shillings I nearly left it, but my blood was up and I didn't.

'Forty-four,' I said, 'and that's the lot.'

It was – down came the hammer and that beautiful little heifer was all mine. I ought to be ashamed to admit this, but for some time after, I couldn't concentrate on the proceedings, much less do it all again. In the next quarter of an hour I went out two or three times to have another look at my heifer, which, if designed as a moral booster backfired badly – she seemed to have grown smaller each time.

Before the day ended however, I had managed to find her a mate, black again but a cow-heifer this time. I won't go through it all again but believe me it was every bit as bad and seemed to drag on forever. A quick dash to beat the crowd to the office, paid my bill (we always paid on the day) then over to the cricket pavilion for a cup of tea and a few minutes of pretend calmness.

I've already stated the enjoyment always derived by the drive to Gloucester and it's true, I did enjoy the ride, but that day the countryside slipped by unnoticed and I arrived home miraculously unscathed with the real trial yet to come. It was little comfort to find that my dad had already gone off racing (Saturdays and Wednesdays) and the verdict would need to wait until next morning.

After breakfast I pushed the door open and shepherded my dad in for the inspection. I'd already told him the prices and he never needed telling twice. He looked them over most carefully, ran a practised hand along each, then stood back for another long look. I caught the cow-heifer in the 'Lichfield George' way and held her mouth open for him to see there were only four broad teeth and four calves' teeth. No trouble on that score, after which came another protracted stare.

'How big's that?' he asked, pointing to the heifer.

'Eight hundredweight.' No hesitation.

'Are you sure?'

'If she's not eight hundredweight, she's eight-and-a-quarter.'

'Are you sure?'

'Positive.'

'Well I'll tell you something. She's not eight hundredweight and she's not eight and a quarter – she weighs nine.'

I looked as hard as I could but she didn't look nine hundredweight to me – and I was prejudiced.

'And I'll tell you something else you don't know – you've bought one heifer and you've got two – the little sod's in-calf.' There was nothing vague about it, no question of her 'might being' in-calf, or 'could be' in-calf. He'd looked at her for a few minutes and that was that – he knew. I'd seen her in the ring, weighed her up, bought her, examined her with love a dozen times since, and the idea hadn't entered my head. It was the same with the weight. He'd seen a heifer that weighed nine hundredweight and that was it.

I should explain that for my heifer to be in-calf was not good news because, for two very good reasons, the Ministry of Food did not accept animals that were pregnant. Firstly, hard-up farmers (and there was never a shortage) might always be tempted to sell their milking cows and create a milk crisis – all farm produce, especially milk and meat was taken much more seriously in those post-war days. Then there was the second consideration, which is slightly more complex. The Ministry grades were based on percentage of dead meat per live hundredweight. If my dad was right (and I knew better than to doubt it), even if my heifer was only three months gone and the calf hardly formed, the weight of water she would be carrying would be enough to alter the percentage balance and make her ungradeable.

The alternative was to keep her until she calved. We were never in the dairy farming business and were not equipped for it, but that wasn't the real problem. Far more important was the fact that the heifer was not much more than a calf herself and was in-calf as the result of an accident – 'stole the bull' is the correct expression; so there was always the chance of things going wrong and losing both mother and calf. (Which is most possibly the reason she found her way to Gloucester in the first place.) Incidentally, the very fact that there was a calf inside would make her weight up to the nine-hundredweight my dad was so confidently expecting.

With my second purchase, the cow-heifer, there was also a slight difference of opinion. This time we agreed on the weight but while I had calculated the grade at 'A minus', my dad thought only 'B plus'. The difference between these grades was a substantial amount, about 12 shillings per hundredweight if I remember correctly, so it was something of a sink-or-swim affair, depending on the graders. The inspection over we turned them both out into the field and all my dad said was, 'We'll see what happens on Wednesday – You'll get yourself into worse messes before you're finished.' I've seen him fly into real tantrums for far less so I suppose I'd been let off lightly – a bit deflating just the same.

Later on we got to discussing Gloucester itself and I told him exactly how things went. I described the thin-faced Frank as best I could but he couldn't place where they'd met. The Harry Wooton bit seemed to surprise him, especially the welcome he'd extended me. Usually when I talked to my dad he only seemed to be half listening, as though his head was so full of other things there was no room to spare (which was most likely the case). But he listened hard to my Wooton epic, really hard, and went back into the house smiling to himself with no intention of sharing the amusement. Had me puzzled for a long time that did.

He set me another puzzle on the following Wednesday and, to tell the truth, I've never been able to solve it. Both my Gloucester cattle were graded with no fuss whatever (and incidentally the heifer weighed nine hundredweights exactly). Now the farmer grader at Barnt Green was a very clever man, make no mistake about that, and also he was a stickler for the rules. What I've never been able to fathom was, did my dad have a quiet word and kid him into grading the heifer, just to encourage me a bit (because it certainly did), or was it a case of 'mugs for luck'?

I will end this passage with a short foot-note of a technical nature and suggest that those uninterested in such things move on to the next chapter and promise they will lose nothing by so doing.

After about six months, the udder of a heifer in-calf for the first time will gently begin to fill out and a sticky substance can be drawn from the teats; although this should be avoided because it can lead to trouble later. In the later period of pregnancy, the calf can actually be felt by gently swaying the stomach from side-to-side (an acquired art admittedly) but in the early stages a really practised eye is called for. The very act of forming a calf calls for some sacrifice on behalf of the mother and it's the loin area that takes the initial punishment. My Gloucester heifer was full-meated with a well-rounded rump and deep set shoulders, but the loins were not up to the standard of the rest – after my dad had pointed it out I could see it for myself. It was not nearly as obvious as this short description might suggest, but for men like Jake it was painted on the wall in letters ten-feet high.

Jim Cook

•

We have to get used to people dropping out of our lives because it's inevitable, but at about the time I started attending Gloucester Market, Jim Cook gave in his notice. It was a shock and a sadness because although he is now the sole survivor from the original set-up he was the first to go. He'd been there right from the beginning, before the beginning in fact. Jim was working this farm when my dad bought it in 1927, so he was sort of taken over, along with a few other fixtures and fittings that happened to be here. After something like twenty-five years he left on a Thursday, and in such a hurry there was no time to say goodbye – how times have changed. Today he'd have been presented with a gold watch and maybe even a Duke of Edinburgh Award.

I can't remember Jim Cook as anything other than a grown man and something of a giant, although when I first knew him he must have been a lad of sixteen or so. In truth he was of average height, five-feet-nine or thereabouts, sturdily built and stronger than he looked although it was probably as much will-power as physical strength. When Jim wanted something to move it usually moved. He was also a creature of extremes, occasional bouts of severe headache could make him somewhat violent, yet in the right mood he was a great chap and we often spent long hours chasing each other round the yard on our bikes when by rights he should have been at home. But I remember him mostly for his absolute fearlessness with animals. Horses or cattle, large or small, all met their match with Jim Cook and it didn't take them long to realise it. There's no room for doubt that that temper of his had something to do with it, but it was results that really mattered and I never saw him beaten.

Take horses for instance.

It's impossible to over-rate the old-time carthorse. They were lovely to look at, cheap to operate, bred their own replacements and fertilised the land at the same time. Much has been said about their ability to pull heavy loads but I still think that only those who have witnessed it at first hand can fully appreciate the brute strength of those flesh and blood traction engines. I've seen laminated leather traces three-inches wide and over an inch thick snap like carrots, and that from a steady pull and no snatching whatever. They were clever enough to wriggle from side-to-side to start a heavy wagon moving The laws of inertia were something they understood at least as well as we did. They were also crafty and given to changes of mood. After working perfectly for an hour or so they'd start weaving about, treading on the crops instead of in between the rows, suddenly veer off toward the home gate or take fright at things they'd walked past hundreds of times – 'acting up' as Jim used to say. At such times he would first coax and pat, then carefully examine for irritation caused by twisted chains or straps, but if all was in order and the behaviour continued, he took a different line altogether. A gnarled left hand would grab the bridle close to the bit, and a heavy right would come swinging across to deliver a couple of smart blows to the snout, and perhaps after a pause another couple.

These weren't children's ponies or anything of the sort. Towering above both of us and plunging and dancing about was something like a ton of quivering horse-flesh. To tell the truth, I never liked those periodic skirmishes. For one thing they used to frighten me and for another, I always thought they'd only make things worse and the horses more unmanageable than ever. But strangely enough they did work, and after Jim had had his say the animals would settle down and give no more trouble for the rest of the day.

To appreciate Jim's handling of cattle it must first be understood that we weren't normal farmers dealing with animals we'd reared ourselves and knew intimately. The lorries backed-up, the ramps came down, and whatever came charging off were ours. Also, it should be pointed out that when a farmer decides to sell cattle, all things being equal, it's the kickers and the awkward devils that go first, so the chances of our getting the docile ones were always less than even. It made no difference. Jim followed them into the buildings, pushed in among them without giving it a thought, wrestled them against the standings and had the chain fastened round their neck before they realised what had happened. Even bullocks and heifers that had never been tied before received the same reckless treatment. After which he pushed his way between them with buckets of food and water twice a day, dodging the hooves by instinct.

If they did manage to kick him, he kicked them back; the ratio being in the order of two to one, depending mainly on how hard the first. Being kicked by cows brings to mind another of those popularly held misconceptions regarding animal behaviour. It's widely believed that cows use their horns and horses their hooves when they wish to register a protest or grievance and it's true – they do both. But in my experience the main thing to watch out for is at the opposite end in both cases. It's cows that do most of the kicking – spiteful horses bite.

Then there's ingenuity, of which Jim Cook had his own special brand. To demonstrate this at best I must go back many years, to the beginning of mechanical road haulage of farm animals. To be precise 'mechanical' is not really appropriate in this instance so I'll say 'forerunner to mechanisation' which should cover it nicely. The contrivance in question had a wooden body, similar in most ways to a modern cattle lorry except for one important item – instead of an engine, it had a pair of shafts and was pulled on its way by a cart horse. I only saw this contraption many years later, by which time it had been reduced to a rotting wreck on our rubbish heap. The one tiny speck of paint still showing told me for certain that it was a dark blue in colour, but that's about all. However, if I scratch a fairly moderate memory fairly hard the name Viking seems to be lurking somewhere, although I don't know how or why.

About two miles south of our village is a well-known beauty spot brought about by a wide view of rolling countryside as seen from the top of a steep (1 in 8) hill. Apart from the actual gradient, this escarpment was the devil to cycle up because its steepest part is almost at the very top. My dad bought a rather large bull from a farmer a mile or so on the downhill side and sent Jim with the horse and cattle float (to give it its correct title) to fetch it home. An hour or so later found Jim with the bull safely loaded and on his way back – James Cook happy in the knowledge that the difficult part was already successfully accomplished.

But about a third of the way up that hill, with every step striking sparks from the tarmac, the old horse began blowing hard, weaving from side to side, and finally came to a shaky halt with only Jim's desperately applied handbrake stopping the whole caboodle from rolling back down, horse and all. I don't know to this day just what I would have done in such circumstances, but there's one thing I'm quite certain about – Jim Cook's solution would never have occurred in a month of Sundays.

Bulls, even your own bulls that are known intimately, are always handled with a certain amount of care – other people's bulls even more so – and this regardless of any soothing claims by their previous owner. The long established method (still in operation as far as I know) was to tie a long rope to the ring in the animal's nose and with this rope threaded through the front of the vehicle, the animal could be coaxed inside without risk of anybody being trapped in that confined space.

Jim climbed down from his perch, opened the ramp and led the bull out onto the road. Then he concocted a sort of harness from the rope, fastened the bull to the front of the shafts, and that was it. Despite the fact that the ramp was left to drag along behind, that old bull pulled both horse and cart to the top of the hill without really trying.

Although I've nearly forgiven him by now, I haven't forgotten that Jim Cook was singularly responsible for the ruination of my very first date. I was fifteen and the girl slightly less at the time, so it would be quite easy to consider it a non-event and hardly worthy of mention in so serious a narrative as this – nothing could be further from the truth. She was lovely and I'd been straining my brains for weeks trying to engineer this date. So much so that, having discovered she attended a tennis club in the village, I enrolled. I didn't understand the game, never having come face to face with a tennis ball, and didn't even own a pair of plimsolls (or pumps as we called them). What a happy chap I was when, after several false starts, I finally got around to asking for this assignation and actually won it.

My dad was in his usual Saturday afternoon position, asleep on the sofa – no problem there. My mother didn't seem to notice that I was somewhat poshed up, and even Laura allowed me to dash through her kitchen without comment (a rare occurrence that) but out in the courtyard with escape more or less an accomplished fact, I ran smack into Jim Cook.

'Where do you think you're going?'

'I'm going out.'

'You're not you know, we're haymaking.'

Now Jim Cook was not a bad chap, and among other things he had a well-developed countryman's sense of humour, but one thing he never joked about was haymaking. Even today, our weather patterns being what they are, haymaking is still a tricky business. Nowadays we have modern machines that can whiz round a hayfield in top gear and shake the hay thoroughly, regardless of how heavy the crop. With only moderate luck, within three or four days of the grass being cut, it is rowed, baled and safely carried and that's that. In the old days it was a most desperate business and no mistake. Jim mowed the grass with a two-horse mower, a highly-skilled operation that I never was entrusted with, and best attempted very early in the morning or at evening time, while the grass was wet with dew. Next came a whole series of tasks, some horse-drawn and the rest all elbow power – I was entrusted with all of them. Even in perfect weather it was a hot, dusty and tiring business that went on for three weeks at a stretch. If the weather turned nasty halfway through, the whole lot needed to be done again, sometimes more than once, and every time the hay got less in weight and lower in quality. Old-time farmers have been known to say that bad hay is so hard to make, it should be worth more than best. So when Jim said there was haymaking to be done I knew he meant it, and in any case, there in the yard stood the two horses, already harnessed and waiting – I was lost and knew it. I did the decent thing and raced off to our meeting place to leave her a note, which must have done the trick because we did eventually get together, although we didn't last long – there's nothing like getting things right first time. I don't know whether that episode has any bearing or not but I still don't like haymaking and am always very glad when it's over and done.

With a father and two or three brothers all farmhands, Jim had no doubt picked up a working knowledge of his trade as a boy, but I've come to realise that, in the main, he must have been self-taught. How else could it have been? He'd spent a large part of his working life with us and there was no-one there who could teach him farm-work. Just the same, there were other things to learn and in the early days my dad took him to the slaughterhouse so that he could kill and dress a cow as well as many who called themselves slaughtermen. This came in very handy because as well as attending race meetings, my dad bred greyhounds, some top-class dogs among them, all groomed, fed, and exercised by the amazing Jim Cook who, as I say, also killed and dressed the odd knacker cow that arrived at the farm especially for the purpose. (I don't think there was anything illegal in this practice as there was never any question of selling the meat, but to be truthful I've never given it a thought until this very minute). I am now going back to when I was a boy of about six or seven and must admit that this killing business upset me at first, but I soon got used to it to the extent that blood became much like sump oil and cow muck – I was never happier than when plastered with either.

The years with Jim Cook are really another story and might one day find themselves in another book, but there is one more activity I must mention because it seemed to be going on continuously. In fact, I'm still called on to do it and think of Jim Cook every time. I refer to the wretched business of mending fences. It has taken me thirty years of dedicated (self-taught) hedgelaying to get this place in order and even now there are the odd dodgy places that lead to the occasional escape and subsequent chase around the district. So it goes without saying that in those days things were rough; rotten old implements tied together with bits of string were often all there was holding us together. But that wasn't the real trouble. The place was never big enough, and my dad was always renting grazing from our neighbours. I always asked the same silly question, 'What are the fences like?' and always got the same answer, 'You might have to slip a bit of wire up here and there.'

That lousy job was not made any better by my dad's lack of interest in farm-work, which was fully reflected in our supply of hand tools. The stakes weren't driven in with a mallet because we hadn't got one, but rather with an iron crowbar six-feet long and two-inches in diameter which Jim swung high above his head and brought crashing down on the stake I was holding. He was good at it mind, never missed, which is just as well otherwise I'd be writing this with my foot.

The saddest part of the story is, though I'll never know for sure, Jim's decision to leave could, in part at least, have been attributed to me – although if that was the case, Hitler also had a hand in it. I say this because, like a lot of others, I came home after three years in the army nursing the ridiculous idea that it would all carry on as though nothing had happened.

What had happened was that either I had forgotten just how shabby and decrepit the farm really was, or I'd carried a mind-picture that had become too bright. In any event, I decided if something wasn't done, and done soon, our poor old farm would crumble into dust and blow away; the cracking barns, the weed-grown yards, the overgrown hedges, the whole neglected lot. I started from the first day and although Jim took a hand there was none of the old enthusiasm, and I knew his heart wasn't in it. My dad stayed unhelpfully neutral but just the same, I knew what he was thinking. He never was a one to go looking for work and his vote would have gone with Jim. As always there was no discussion and no consultation. My dad carried on with the business-end and left us both to it, although the roles had become reversed. Now it was me who found the jobs and Jim who helped me to do them. And all the time, a silent, creeping misery was settling over a place that had always been too busy and too happy to grant it room. There's always the chance that I've read things into the situation that were never there in the first place. It could be that Jim had been here too long already and was overdue for a change, in which case I've assumed myself guilty for nothing.

Anyway, the rest has already been said, he gave in his notice and left, took a job away from farming and stayed there until he retired (last year). After him there was a constant stream of farmhands whose stay ranged from four years to two weeks. One or two were good, some were all right, and some no use at all, but among the lot there was not another Jim Cook, nor anything even vaguely resembling one.

A Misadventure

·

The City of Birmingham has sprawled ever nearer until, by now, our village has been more or less gobbled up, from a character point of view that is, although we're still waiting for the buses and other amenities that were supposed to be the good side of being hugged close to the chest of the big city. During, and for a few years after the war however, it was still a village in the old style; two policemen, three pubs, a Jubilee tree, a blacksmith, and the normal quota of idiots (about four). There was also a handful of men who saw themselves individually as the village squire; mainly – I strongly suspect – because, through indolence or lethargy, their families had hardly set foot outside the parish boundary for several generations. Yet the man I always thought of in that dignified role was disqualified on all counts, not that it bothered him over-much because, along with my dad, he was one of the most non-political men in the area (and probably the county).

Jethro Tate lived in a beautifully renovated old house standing in a few acres, located about two miles outside the village to the south. Handsome, well-educated (Cambridge I think), always immaculate and a director of more than one company that have since become household names. Not only was he a non-villager, the Tate family were newcomers having resided in our village a mere six years (I write now of 1947), but by the time he retired, a year or two ago, and they moved out to find some sun, his qualifications were much better. Another few years and he might truly have become one of us.

One evening, in the summer of 1947, a highly-polished voice came down our telephone to inform my dad that its owner was looking for a milking cow and would he kindly send one on, black and white for preference, and that was the start of a most unlikely alliance that lasted for years. My dad not only found a cow and delivered it, he adopted Jethro Tate on the strength of it, keeping a maternal eye on the cow and her off-springs, which were left entirely to his judgement and marketed at his discretion. I don't know just what they found to talk about, being almost diametrically opposites, yet Jethro was singled out for a very high honour indeed. He was the only man I ever knew my dad to call on for a friendly visit and no other reason.

I watched all this from a distance, as it were, because despite the infinitesimal amount of buying and selling involved, it wasn't really part of the business but something separate. If there's any validity in the theory that we all keep secret gardens, I'll risk sounding ridiculous by saying that Jethro Tate's milking cow was possibly my dad's. By 1953, she'd been in residence for six years, had five calves, and was about ten-years old. She'd also fallen victim to some of the normal catastrophes that bedevil milking cows, cut teats, mastitis, rheumatism, and was beginning to look a little the worse for wear. In short, it was time for her to go, but as this was very much a non-agricultural set-up there were unusual complications. Jethro Tate saw fit not to tell his family what was afoot and instead, they all went off for a long weekend while the deed was being done. A cloak and dagger affair for the best possible motives. He also asked my dad to make arrangements for the cow to be killed at home, rather than be taken away alive.

The trouble was that although my dad assured Jethro he'd attend to everything as requested I knew, and my dad knew, that he'd do no such thing. When it came to cattle and meat my dad was a professional's professional, and anything he was to be party to needed doing right. Jethro was a good friend and certainly meant well but he didn't realise what he was asking my dad to do.

To call in a knackerman to shoot and make off with a perfectly good cow was like asking my dad to chop off one of his fingers. In his book knackermen were like doctors, very useful when you needed them. What good a knackerman's miserable £15 for an animal worth three times as much? Who in his right mind sends for a doctor when nobody's ill? 'I'm very sorry Jethro old son,' I thought when my dad explained the situation, 'but my dear old dad isn't going to stand for that.' And of course he wasn't. On the Friday of the arranged weekend I was instructed to go to Jethro's place after Gloucester, the next day, and take the cow to Birmingham abattoir. (I should explain there was a system in operation throughout the period whereby farmers could have animals killed in this way. It was really designed specifically for emergencies and called appropriately enough the Casualty Dept., although animals didn't need to be victims of road accidents to be eligible. The meat was then allocated according to its quality and the owner received payment on a deadweight basis).

That should have been the end of the story, but I'm afraid it wasn't. After a day at Gloucester (Harry Wooton and all that) and a hundred-odd mile round trip, followed by something of a scuffle to single-handedly load the cow at Tate's place, I wasn't in the best of form by the time I arrived at the abattoir. I didn't back the lorry in far enough or square enough, and didn't fix the side gates firm enough, and would you believe, old Jethro's pet cow escaped and set off through the streets of Birmingham with myself coming up behind. By that time it was half-past eight with the sun and the moon both visible in the sky and about as bright as each other. There followed a most wearying pursuit through the twilight streets of Birmingham, starting from Bromsgrove Street and zigzagging in a roughly southerly direction. We went under two old railway arches, or perhaps it was the same one twice – she kept doubling back, determined to confuse the issue. I almost got up alongside of her twice, but the old devil dug up some extra energy and put a spurt on, leaving me back in second place. There were plenty of people about and the streets were full of motors (Saturday night remember), but either they couldn't see an old black and white cow ambling along a few feet ahead of a chap with a stick, or they thought we were just a couple of cranks who did that sort of thing every Saturday night. No-one raised so much as a finger.

About three miles, and half-an-hour away from the abattoir, after continuously moving due south at a jog-trot, she suddenly veered straight across the road and shot up a factory alley; good news in fact, because there was a gate to it that I dragged to before continuing the chase. What came next was a surprise and a shock even to me, and believe it or not I'd been on a few capers of that sort over the years. The driveway opened up into several yards and enclosures, all strewn with wooden crates and boxes. I followed the racket as she cannoned into these obstacles, getting more excited by the second, until I saw her galloping figure at the far end of the yard, and directly to her front, was a cast-iron, open-treaded fire escape. She neither checked nor hesitated, up those steep steps she went, all three flights, until she came to rest at the very top, the clouds of steamy breath and all her white areas picked out quite clearly in the moonlight.

I went back for the lorry and she was still standing on that narrow platform when I returned, realising no doubt by then, just what a mess she'd gotten us both into. I backed the lorry right to the bottom of the fire escape, dropped the ramp and opened the side-gates, but because the side-gates of a cattle lorry are shorter than the ramp, there were spaces at each side. I did not want another chase around the town, so I spent some time dragging and stacking some of those boxes to fill the gaps at either side. All that was needed now was to coax her back down, and for the benefit of those who don't know, four-legged animals do not like going downhill, even forwards and on grass, let alone backwards and on cast-iron stairs.

Had she been a big cow it might have been a real catastrophe. The whole framework could have collapsed or pulled away from the wall. Comparatively speaking, that old factory was on a par with Jethro's cow as regards age and condition. As it was, she was about nine hundred-weight, which was bad enough; she filled the platform completely and with most of her weight and bulk above the handrail, making it impossible to squeeze past from behind. Once that deep in trouble however, a bit more couldn't make much difference. I 'broke and entered' from the floor below, groped my way about until back at the top – on the right side of the cow, but the wrong side of the door. Fortunately it was secured with bolts which I drew, eased open the door and there I was, face-to-face with Jethro's cow, both perched high above the sleeping roof tops of down-town Birmingham. A narrow, rusty, twisting stairway was the only road back to the lorry, a black shadow far below.

She couldn't have turned around even if she'd wanted to. Her body filled the space between the handrails. There was only one action I could take so I hit her on her nose with the flat of my hand. She began to back down. The whole manoeuvre was scary and no mistake, but at full forty feet above the ground that first leg was the worst. For some of the time she went steadily down from one step to the next like the gentle old lady I'd always mistaken her for, but now and again, she'd slip between the open steps, then she'd panic and start the whole assembly shaking. Once or twice there was a real danger of her rolling right over, which must have brought the whole lot crashing down, and me with no option but to keep on after her, tapping away at that nose, otherwise I'm quite sure she would have ran right back to the top. Two things I now know for certain. I must have been quite off my rocker to even attempt it, and wouldn't do the same today for all the rice in China. Today I'd do like everybody else and ring the fire brigade.

Straight into the lorry she went – once we'd reached the ground that is – and by the time I'd travelled a few hundred yards I couldn't help but see the funny side of it, although I said nothing to the gateman at the abattoir nor to my dad the next morning. I watched the *Birmingham Mail* very closely for the next few days but found no mention of any phantom burglar, which I still think strange to say the least. I'd left one window broken and open, the door at the top of the stairs ajar, cow muck all over the fire escape. God knows how much damage among the crates and things in the yard, and in those days we like to think that vandalism and crime was not the everyday occurrence it has since become. Yet no-one seems to have noticed anything and certainly not the eyes and ears of the *Birmingham Evening Mail*.

I hoped that was the end of the story as indeed it was, although in the cattle business nothing is ever certain. My dad found a replacement that soon settled down under the care of Jethro's handyman-gardener, a kind little Jersey cow this time. I could almost have tucked her under my arm and carried her down that fire escape. Just the same my prayers went something like this. That those two old pals have a fall-out before the next ten years was up, or else my dad decides to forego his principles and allow the poor old knackerman a few cheap quid next time and leave me out of it.

Christmas Show 1954

Percy Tricklebank tidying up the front row of beef. The tails and tassels were part of the Christmas fancy dressing.

Trouble

·

To arrive late at a cattle market was bad enough. For one thing, it upset my dear old dad. 'Where the bloody hell have you been?' When often as not he knew, because he'd sent me there himself. To arrive late at Stratford was even worse. At Stratford there was a real power-jet washing hose against which the most mid-summer baked-on cow muck stood no chance whatever. (I sometimes dream about that hose pipe even now.) So the day I turned up at Stratford in time to miss the sale completely, no chores done, no wash-out, and no bit of paper with the cow-heifer numbers for my dad, had got to portend evil doings in the near future – nothing was ever surer. I was annoyed with myself on principle because there's nothing I find more aggravating than tearing about trying to catch myself up, especially on a market day, which was usually full to the brim anyway. There stood my dad just outside the office door checking through his bills, and when he saw me a whole mass of minor irritations chased each other across his screwed-up face, all trying to be first. After a greeting I well remember but won't repeat, he said:

'You know where Johnson's place is don't you?'

I'd been there a few dozen times, so I said I did.

'There's a bunch of heifers in the stores. Get the tickets off and take eight of 'em there straight away. Leave the knacker, that's for Charlie.'

'Store cattle' I should explain, are young animals for feeding on and supplying stores to farmers was another of our sidelines. In fact, in the spring and early summer it could amount to half our turnover. They are not sold singularly like fat cattle but rather in 'bunches' and a bunch of stores can be anything from four to forty. So in view of the outcome of this particular transaction, I think it important to point out at least one of the intricacies of the store cattle business.

When faced with the problem of making up bunches of stores for sale, some men take great pains to ensure that the finished collection all match each other as to age, size, and condition, and are in fact a 'matching bunch'. There are those however who don't see it in quite the same way, because as the bunch are all to be sold at the one price, the temptation arises to smuggle the odd inferior animal in with the others. The process is known as 'mixing' and although it works often enough, it can also backfire very badly. There's no law against a prospective buyer pointing out the 'mixer' and kicking up such a fuss that the opposition is put off – 'crabbing' they call it. With men like my dad there was no danger of the 'mixer' being overlooked, but rather 'over-compensated for'.

Off we went to the store pens to find our bunch, nine in all, shorthorn heifers and about eighteen-months old. They were what we call 'out-lyers' which simply means they'd spent the winter out of doors and now, with the warmer weather, their long winter coats had started coming off in patches, so that they closely resembled a platoon of badly shell-shocked soldiers. Scruffy is the word for all nine, but one in particular was even scruffier than the rest. She was smaller and skinnier than her mates, and her tail and hind quarters were coated with excrement, a sure sign of Johnes Disease, a wasting diarrhoea, probably the knackerman's best friend. (This affliction was quite common in those times. Thankfully it has become somewhat rare today but is still about, and my vet tells me that even with our collection of modern antibiotics it is not easy to cure). Just to be on the safe side, my dad pointed her out two or three times, unnecessarily and for aggravation purposes. I might have been late but I wasn't blind and there really was no danger of Charlie getting the wrong one. Charlie, incidentally, was one of our tame knackermen.

Johnson's farm was some six miles from Stratford and the next half-hour was taken up loading the stores and dashing them over there, normally one of my harmless pleasures on account of Farmer Johnson's three lovely daughters. That day it should have been even more pleasing because he was very happy with the heifers and invited me in for a cup of tea, but there was much left to do and my dad waiting at Stratford Market, so I had to turn him down – yet another good reason for my disliking being late.

I snatched an hour or so on the Thursday morning for a spot of overdue maintenance on the Ford and was still at it when my dad set off for Banbury, the big day of the week. About to get into his car he turned: 'You'll get there before the end won't you?' – absolutely uncalled-for and unnecessary, although it was the sort of thing my dad was good at and I was expecting it, '...and don't forget Charlie's 'Johnah' (cattleman's term for sufferers of Johne's Disease). Another attempt to enter the car and then, 'and don't leave it hanging about in the market, drop it off in one of the railway pens – Charlie tells me there's a war on.' There was no need for any of that either because it was all normal practice – even the 'war news' was standard. Wherever there were two knackermen within striking distance of each other you had a ready-made recipe for warfare, especially if they were sizeable operators, mainly because knackermen are never above treading on each others toes when it comes to Zoo contracts and the like. Incidentally the reason the heifer was going to Banbury was because that was Charlie's territory, his main camp being situated in the next town, some eight miles away.

Banbury is about the same distance from our farm as Gloucester – fifty miles or so, only to the south-west rather than the south-east. It was a pleasant journey devoid of urban areas and in fact, for me, the ride was the best part of what was otherwise a long and tiring day. I arrived there at about eleven o'clock; unloaded Charlie's heifer in the railway pen then dashed off to the wash to do the scrubbing out I hadn't managed on the Tuesday. For what it's worth the wash at Banbury was every bit as good as the one at Stratford, only there was usually a queue for it and it cost a shilling. I had a look round for Charlie or his man without finding either, carried out the search for calves' teeth, had a sort of wash (red hot water, no soap, and paper towel) then went to the sale ring, handed my dad his piece of paper and sat watching the sale, although not for long. Some fifteen minutes later, one of the clerks came to tell me I was wanted in the auctioneer's office.

Standing by the office door was a complete stranger, Wellingtons, grey flannels (baggy at the knees) shabby old sports jacket, battered green trilby and, I think, a moustache. If he looked like anything at all it was a fisherman of the rod-and-line variety. He nodded when the clerk introduced me, asked me to 'come with him' and we set off across the sale yard without another word, with at least one of us having no idea as to the purpose of our trip. Jim Cook used to say that horses could smell trouble and I believed him because he knew about such things, but it wasn't till then that I realised I was similarly gifted.

On that silent walk I caught a strong niff of the stuff and it got stronger by the yard. By the time we were standing by the railway pen and looking at Charlie's heifer, I'd decided just what heading it came under. He wasn't a fisherman at all. He worked for the railway and Charlie's heifer was trespassing on their property without a ticket.

'Does that beast belong to you?'

'Yes.' Although it didn't. It was my dad's.

'You're Harry Shutkever?'

'You know I am.' He had a pad in his hand and was writing in it.

'Address?' It was trouble all right; the question was how much?

He finished the long, silent job of writing my address down in his pad, all in block capitals, then stood for a moment or two looking slant-eyed and hard, between the fence rails at the heifer. His attitude was not officious but it wasn't friendly either. The best I could make of it was that he was taking himself and his job far more seriously than the situation warranted.

'Have you owned her long?'

'Two days actually.' The truth never hurt anyone.

'Where did she come from?' There was something wrong somewhere. What business was that of the railway?

'Who wants to know?'

'I do.'

'And who might you be?'

'I'm an RSPCA Inspector.' My nose had been right, but that hadn't stopped it leading me up a gum tree.

I don't remember the rest of the inquisition, not in so many words, but he kept insisting that the animal was in a distressed condition, unfit to travel, and trying to get me to admit it. Needless to say, I let him down, first because I wasn't that daft, and second because it wasn't true. She was a 'Johnah' and on the way to the knacker yard, she was wasting away with disease and not a healthy animal. But she was not distressed, not in any pain, and if we had opened the gate she would have chased around the sale yard as well as any of the others. And he knew it. He didn't get worked up or excited and in fact didn't raise his tone at all, although the same can't be said of myself. After about ten minutes I'd had enough.

'You wanted to know where she came from – well I'll tell you. Two days ago she was in Stratford Market. There's an RSPCA inspector on duty there, and what's more he's in uniform, not masquerading as a civilian. If that heifer is unfit to travel now she couldn't have been any better then. Tell me Mr Whatever-your-name-is, why didn't he say something?'

'I'm not interested in what happened two days ago. Your beast is unfit to travel and she won't leave this yard alive. And furthermore the matter won't rest there.'

'You do whatever you think fit. I've got better things to do than stand about arguing with trumped-up idiots like you!'

The fate of the heifer made little difference as far as we were concerned. Charlie's man turned up and instead of taking her away alive, he shot her and winched her into his wagon – dead. I went back to the sale ring and told my dad the whole miserable story. It shook him a bit and he didn't try to hide it He always avoided trouble with officialdom and had taught me to do likewise. Nevertheless he found nothing to complain about in what I'd said – and I gave it to him chapter and verse – and I'm quite sure that had he been there instead of me that inspector's ride would have been infinitely rougher. In fact he said as much.

What had really happened was that the Banbury knackerman's war had flared up into open conflict. Somehow or other, Charlie's rival had spotted the heifer, traced it back to me and worked the rest out for himself. It was no secret that we were agents for Charlie. It had been going on for years (and carried on afterwards). All it needed was a snide whisper to the RSPCA that a 'distressed animal' was standing in the railway pen and they, in the person of my fisherman, decided to make a case of it.

We were summoned to appear in Banbury courthouse a few weeks later and didn't have a prayer. To people unused to cattle dealers and markets, the very mention of cruelty to animals was enough to see us hanged – and the solicitor for the RSPCA was taking no chances.

'…Every bony prominence was bruised and bleeding…' and the only effective evidence to the contrary had long since been killed and eaten by the lions.

We were judged guilty and fined twenty pounds.

How guilty we really were is, I think, best judged by the attitude of the people in the trade. From what I've already written it should be evident that they were (and still are) a very down-to-earth lot, and in the chapters to come this message will become stronger. They miss nothing that happens in and around cattle markets and remember it all forever. Most of the nick-names I mentioned earlier stemmed from incidents that occurred long years past; the man who transformed cows into cow-heifers (twenty-five years ago) is still referred to by some as 'the dentist'. Yet, neither in the immediate future nor at any time since has there ever been mention of that incident, and I'm quite certain I am the only living person who has bothered to remember it.

There were two incidents on that day in Banbury court which, although somewhat irrelevant to the story, I think are worth including.

Our solicitor was a white-haired, distinguished-looking senior partner in a very respectable Birmingham law firm. He put our case over in an extremely able manner and took his time about it, so that there was a lunch recess before the final judgement. We sat about after having eaten and were waiting for the proceedings to re-open with the opposing counsel (also distinguished-looking, although considerably younger) standing nearby. Our man then stepped across, shook him by the hand, and although I am making up the actual words, the gist of their conversation went something like this.

'That was a good point you made about the time factor. Put me in mind of "Jones versus Jones" at Exeter 1922.' A pause then ensued whilst he thumbed through his several books and a further silent moment while both men studied.

'No. Actually it was from "Smith versus Smith" 1870,' at which one of his books became the object of deep study. This went on for several minutes after which, with another handshake, they parted company.

Looking back, I now see it as no more than a display of civilised professionalism, although who they were trying to impress I wouldn't know. At the time, to uneducated peasants the like of Shutkever and Son, they seemed more like two men enjoying a game of chess and we were the matchsticks they were playing for.

The second occurred on the way back to Birmingham, and considering the time that had been wasted, the utter nonsense of the case itself and the miserable outcome, it could easily be the dearest bit of free advice ever given. I was driving, and our solicitor leaned forward from his seat in the back.

'I'm going to tell you something young man and I want you never to forget it. Should you ever find yourself in trouble of any sort you should make no statement whatever. It might appear that by refusing to speak you are incriminating yourself, but it's not so, and makes the job of your defending counsel that much easier. All you should do is remain calm and say, "I'm sorry, but at this point I have nothing to say."'

Happily, up till now, I have never had the need to put his theory to the test – but I certainly haven't forgotten it.

Chapter Nine

My Own Name

•

My dad was obsessed with the idea that I stand or fall by my own effort and when men like him want something to happen badly enough it usually does. By the April of the following year (1951), progress was such that, having first paid his accountant a fee of twenty-five pounds for the privilege, I had the heartbreaking pleasure of presenting the Inland Revenue with a massive £120. This leaves us with a classic case of principles being at cross purposes, whilst the fact that I was capable of earning money was worth more to my dad than the money itself, he viewed income tax in much the same way as I saw baked-on cow muck – a thing to be avoided as much as possible.

Once again he was to prove himself equal to the occasion, and in an amazingly short time. Less than five minutes after I showed him the taxman's demand he pointed out a serious flaw in the system (not the taxman's, our own). Even my old dad was prepared to admit that I hadn't done too badly. There'd have been no need to part with the £120 otherwise, but in one important aspect I had done it off his back. It was his land I was using and paying no rent and although, to be sure, most of the mileage the Ford was clocking up was on his behalf, all the petrol pumped into the tank was also his. In short, I was cheating both my dad and myself by a bogus shortage in my running expenses. Not just bending the rules, but bending them in the wrong direction. I'm happy to report that I found an honourable way around that dilemma almost by myself.

By then I had built up a useful connection with some of the local farmers on my own account – my farmers rather than my dad's, and although they might not have been aware of it, I treated them in much the same way as a door-to-door salesman his clients. I would 'call in while passing' usually with the old chestnut of being 'short of cattle'. I dropped in on one such farmer, a chap not much older than myself, to be told that he was giving up the farm at the end of the present rent year. It appeared he was never a full tenant, but rather had farmed his 220 acres at a low rent on the written understanding that, given a year's notice he must leave. This was true enough, but, as it happened, not the full story. I discovered later that he was, in fact, two years behind with his rent, but the result was the same. In five month's time, the farm would fall vacant.

The interesting bit was that the landlords were the local council and one of my dad's old cronies had served on that same council for many years. He came back with the information that the land would be needed for development in the near future, but he didn't know when. His advice was that we should take it, so with only the teeniest bit of string-pulling, I became an even more temporary tenant on those same two-hundred-and-twenty acres, and at an even lower rent. Complete autonomy was now almost achieved, and only one further item remained. Having managed to do my own buying from the start, my dad thought it high time I went my own way at the selling end, so within days of establishing myself with my own land – which sounds far grander than it actually was – I started attending a different Ministry grading centre. It was on a Monday and although no great distance from home, about six miles, same as Barnt Green, it carried all the potential terror of another foray into deepest Indian Territory. I won't describe the place in detail because, generally speaking, it was Barnt Green all over again. I'll say only that what happened there shortly after was to trigger off an explosion, the shock-waves of which were never to completely die away.

In the meantime, everything carried on as before. I still attended all the sales with my dad, including Barnt Green Collecting Centre, and still did most of his transport for free (as it turned out). On Mondays, having sorted, transported, and graded my cattle – and sometimes a few for my dad, I chased off to Lichfield to seek out calves' teeth in the running battle to forestall and defeat the antics of friend George, the difference now being that in the unlikely event of our making off with a cow-heifer, I was allowed to cross it off my dad's bill and take to it myself.

Only in the farming were the rules of autonomy allowed to lapse. I had taken on a farmhand of my own, but was still left in charge of operations at home, so now all three of us would gang up on the work in both places; pooling such things as tractors, implements and the like. Incidentally, the horses had now gone. Mainly because there was no longer time to spare for the old ways, but also because, with the going of Jim Cook, it became impossible to find men who could cope with them.

Those were busy, exciting, and challenging times and without a shadow of doubt the big day of the week as far as I was concerned was Saturday. I went to Gloucester every week, ostensibly to find a bargain or two from among the cattle pens, but what I was really doing was 'winning my wings' and couldn't get there fast enough to find the next test.

At all cattle markets there was an element of fun. Ribald comments and cat-calls were constantly bandied about and it was not unknown for an auctioneer to pause in his selling to join in himself. At Gloucester it seemed to go a stage further. There was a carefree atmosphere that I freely admit had me fooled for several weeks. The casual observers watching the proceedings from outside the ring could have been excused for going away with the impression that nobody was interested in the cattle and only made the journey for the laughs. Needless to say, that wasn't the case at all. I soon discovered that the frivolity was no more than a smoke screen, a means of creating confusion, and that the one's doing most of the clowning were the keenest of the lot. The only difference between Gloucester and the other markets was that here, there were a few more clowns than usual and they were better at it. Nevertheless, they were a friendly bunch and certainly a big improvement on the bandits of Lichfield, yet even the friendliness was not quite what it looked. It took some sorting to discover who were friendly with who, and among them were those who hated the sight of one another. Take Taffy Evans, for instance, a cattle buyer who not surprisingly hailed from Cardiff.

Taffy was a good-looking man in his forties with a swashbuckling air, plenty to say for himself and, as he was always in the thick of the fun, could quite easily have been mistaken for a leading member of the glee club. However, Taffy's problem was that he was a physical coward, so that while he was quite a respectable judge of cattle, he was at the same time frightened of them, and believe me, at a place like Gloucester Market, that could be a real handicap. Hatchet-faced Frank waited for a nervous looking animal to come into the ring, carefully manoeuvred it in Taffy's direction, then gave it a sharp jab in the ribs with his cane and shouted, 'Look out Taff!' It's the biggest wonder in the world there was never a serious accident, because if the bullock didn't do it, the way the strung-up Welshman swung his arms and stick about as he jumped clear, could quite easily have knocked an eye out.

If that sounds a bit dangerous, there was another little trick that bordered on being lethal. In the weeks prior to Guy Fawke's Night, the confusion-mongers turned to fireworks and every now and again there'd be an almighty bang right there, in among the cattle. By the end of the day it was sometimes difficult to see across the ring for cordite smoke and what with the general coughing and spluttering and Taffy Evans shouting for a policeman, the poor old auctioneer had his work cut out making himself heard at all. I'm not exaggerating. Believe me, they were just like a bunch of school kids. You would attempt to step across the ring for a better view of an animal and find it impossible, because someone had sneaked up behind and tied your coat tail to the railings. But like I said, it wasn't the innocent fun it appeared because, all the time, cattle were being sold and someone was busy buying them.

For all that, the Gloucester Gang were more likeable rogues than actual villains, and I made some good friends among them; Frank of the hatchet face being one of the best. Then there was Harry Wooton. A busy man was Harry, self-made like my dad, and every bit as hard. Yet he always found time for a word or two, and sometimes his encouragement took a more practical turn. I stood one day and watched him buy a big, clumsy-looking bullock which to my mind was very cheap, and after the sale we were gathered around the canteen counter, drinking tea, when he happened to remark on how dear the cattle had been – which was perfectly true. One way or another, the prices were generally high.

'Don't you like your day's work then, Harry?' My question was not meant to be taken seriously, just friendly comment morelike.

'No I don't. Look at 'em. There's a whole pen-full there that won't earn a tosser between the lot of 'em.'

'Oh, I wouldn't say that myself. There's one there I wouldn't mind giving a bit of profit on.'

'Which one's that?'

'The Friesian bullock towards the end – £62 wasn't it?'

Harry turned to the others who were standing around, also indulging in the tea-drinking ritual. 'Did you hear that, chaps? This fellow here wants to give me some profit on my old bullock.'

'If he's got a fiver to spare he can have all mine.' That was Frank and a picture of misery he looked. 'Wish I'd stopped in bed with the missus now. She wanted me to.'

'Come on lad,' said Harry, 'let's go and have a look.'

'So you think he's cheap do you?' he asked, after we'd studied the bullock in silence. 'How much were you thinking of offering?'

'Well, a few minutes ago I'd have said a fiver, but between the lot of you you've put me off – what about a quid?'

He stood there stroking his chin and looking from me to the bullock and back. 'A quid's no good to you or me lad, so I'll tell you what we'll do. You take the bullock and get him graded. We'll be partners.'

We were to do that several times, and every time I earned profit, which of course, we shared, fifty-fifty – after I'd deducted a few shillings for expenses. 'Standing in' is the correct term for it. Yet every time I told my dad about Harry Wooton, and what he'd done, he refused to share in my enthusiasm for the man. Eventually he came out with his version of what was going on, and there's no doubting the fact that one of us had got it wrong.

'Harry Wooton's a cunning old bugger, take it from me. I've known him for years. He wouldn't see a blind man across the street. He's doing it just to nark me, show me how much money he's making – he's teasing you lad, you just haven't got the brains to see it. But watch him, he gets as jealous as Hell – it's all right now because you're only playing at it, you don't count. Just you wait till you start earning some real money out of Gloucester. That's when you'll find out what sort of a pal Harry Wooton is.'

An account of this nature would be worthless if not kept scrupulously honest. The truth is that at that precise moment I did my dad a serious injustice by suspecting that the boot was on the other foot, and that it was him who was a bit put out by my managing to earn money without his help when he thought I couldn't. Luckily, I held my peace and he never knew of such thoughts. I just carried on and took no notice. While things remained as they were, what my dad thought of Harry Wooton was his business.

For reasons best known to themselves, the graders at Barnt Green did not like grading cows. It might have been a silly sort of snobbery or perhaps even that they didn't understand cows; whatever the reason, it was a fact. They couldn't actually refuse because they were only ministry officials implementing a government scheme, but they could, and did, offer grades that were so low that cows found their way to other collecting centres. As it happened, my dad had always catered for the quality end of the market, so Barnt Green suited his book and he bought only bullocks, heifers, cow-heifers, and top quality cows, with which even the Barnt Green squad could find no fault. At other collecting centres, however, the situation was different, and for those who could handle the lower grade of cows, there was big money to be made. An example of what I'm trying to say would be as follows (the prices are approximate).

The lowest grade for cows (at that time) was B minus and the Ministry price paid was about three pounds per hundredweight, so if the graders accepted a ten-hundredweight cow, it would come to £30. If, however, they were to shake their heads at it, that same cow would be worth little more than knackermeat price. The point is that a man who could get a low-quality cow graded, when others could not, could buy at little over dog-meat price and sell at £3 per hundredweight.

Fortunes were made doing just that, and where big money can be made without actually working, there's usually a villain or two lurking about. The method used was really just another conversion job, similar in some respects to the two mentioned earlier, but certainly far more complex.

In order to be considered gradeable, a cow that weighs 10 hundredweight alive, must produce a meat carcass weighing at least 560 – 610lb, because the basic percentage laid down by Ministry of Agriculture for a cow to be acceptable was 55%. The problem arises when that 10-hundredweight cow is not meaty enough to produce a 560lb carcass. With no way of suddenly increasing the meat content of the animal, the obvious answer is to reduce its live weight so that it then conforms to the Ministry's stipulated 55%. This meant doctoring the weigh-scales at the grading centre or sweetening the clerks who were booking the weights, and, of course, the graders, who were well aware of what was going on. All this illegality called for a considerable amount of corruption, and in considerably high places.

But with my dad's already stated aversion to the basic systems of corruption, and handicapped by an inborn honesty of which I'm not ashamed, competing with well-established villains called for different tactics. So after watching a considerable herd of very poor specimens being accepted by the graders, I walked up to them and pointed out that I was aware of what was going on. I also made a strong point of stating that I would follow up today's cattle and kick-up a real stink at the abattoir, unless my own cattle received similar treatment at their hands.

It's called blackmail – and it works.

A farmer offered me a cow roughly in the aforementioned category and I gave him £18 for it, mainly because it looked big enough, but also because he wouldn't take a penny less. On the Monday I loaded it along with the cattle for grading. The general scheme being to take it on to Lichfield and 'pitching' it onto friend George, or any other mug that happened along. But being a bit short of cattle, genuinely, as it happened, I numbered it up with the rest and let it go through at my grading centre. On that very week, a new grade for low-quality cows had been introduced called M, which stood for 'manufacturing' (sausages and pies), and the price paid was £2.50 per hundredweight. Everybody knew about it, but I hadn't studied the details because, as I say, it was not our normal line of business. The graders poked my cow about a bit and then offered the new M grade, and as she weighed over eleven-hundredweight and was coming to something above £30, I accepted, and very nice too I thought. And I also decided, there and then, that it was time to capitalise on my recent involvement in the villains' club.

The following Saturday found me in Gloucester Market looking for bullocks and heifers as ever, but now the target had become somewhat enlarged because in amongst those pens full of cattle there must surely be one or two more like my 'M' cow. It took till the middle of the morning, because I'm a slow starter at most things, but then, sure enough, I landed one and, as always, Harry Wooton came lumbering over with a word of encouragement.

'Don't worry about that old granny you've just bought, lad. It'll earn a bloody sight more than all your bullocks and heifers, you see if it doesn't.' And later in the day, when I managed to capture another, Harry's few words were similarly encouraging. Naturally enough, my dad took a keen, if sometimes brutally critical interest in all my buying activities and a Sunday morning ritual had come into being which entailed a trip over to my new estate to scrutinise my purchases most thoroughly. Ugly, bony-hipped, heavily-uddered, my two old grannies stood out among a field-full of bullocks and heifers, like a couple of motor accidents. Needless to say, they drew my dad like a fly to a honey-pot. Yet after looking them over for a bit, his remarks weren't directed at the cows' physical deficiencies as was usually the case.

'I'll bet your old pal Harry had something to say about them?'

'Well, he did say how cheap they were.'

'That all?'

'Yes.'

'Both times?'

'Both times.' That was all that was said and we moved on to study the rest. He didn't even think to tell me whether he agreed with Harry Wooton or not, and I didn't ask.

Over the next few weeks it gently built up until I was handling five or six M-type cows per week, and doing very nicely out of them. They didn't all come from Gloucester. There was no danger of that little number lying neglected and I was searching everywhere for them. But the ones that did come out of Gloucester never failed to draw a comment from Harry Wooton. It occurred to me that my dad's views were playing on my mind, to the extent that I was reading too much into what could easily have been no more than the friendly interest he had shown from the first. In any event, I did the right thing and went on laughing, buying, and earning, and left the politics to look after themselves.

The cattle business is really an extension of farming and naturally enough, it's governed by the seasons. Cattle that have been grazing all summer get fat by the autumn and start piling into the markets from about the end of September, right through till Christmas. This busy period is called the 'back end', and it's the time to make money because once it's over and winter sets in, there are several months when it's considered moderately successful just to break even.

The back-end of 1951 was no different from all the others, and by mid-October, Gloucester Market was brim-full, to the extent that we were asked to remove our cattle as soon as possible to make room for those still arriving. The buying technique was not to hurry because, as the day went on and the buyers' needs began to fill, prices were sure to drop. Yet on the fatal day I am about to describe I had bought half-a-dozen cattle in the first twenty minutes, and was looking about for a money-spinning cow or two. All this occurred over thirty year's ago, and could harbour the odd inaccuracy or slight fading with age, but the next bit most certainly does not. I can see it all now, fresh and clear as the day it happened.

A big, deep red cow came into the ring, old as a man and two dogs, and with one horn stuck up in the air and the other curled round her head, a twin sister to the one that jumped over the moon. She was certainly gradeable and if she didn't weigh twelve-hundredweight, she weighed more. I started the bidding at twenty pounds and in the choked-up atmosphere of the day, nobody seemed particularly interested. At £24 the bids had all but stopped, and I had my book in hand ready to write her in. Then, it suddenly took off and I chased it up to £28.75 and stopped. The hammer came down at £29 and the name the auctioneer called out was 'Wooton'. It could easily have been an accident. With all the bustle going on, Harry might not have known who it was he was bidding on, and even when it happened twice more, I was still prepared to give it the benefit of the doubt – something like Chamberlain at Munich, I suppose.

But it didn't stop. I bought a few bullocks and heifers without any trouble, but no cows, not a single one. Every time I bid for a cow, Harry Wooton topped me and bought it.

'What's up, Harry?' I'd asked the question casually enough, the last thing I wanted was to precipitate anything, but believe me, if I'd just bitten his ear off, the reaction could not have been more violent. Harry Wooton rounded on me, red in the face, and I swear his hair was bristling.

'I've had about enough of you.' The voice had boomed out for all to hear. 'You come sneaking into my market and expect me to stand about all day and watch you pinch everything. You're a bloody sight worse than your old man – piss off and find your own markets, or else stop here and help yourself and I'll do the same.' His exact words from nearly thirty years ago. I'll never forget them.

I walked away and left it. I was upset and disappointed, more than a little frightened and don't mind admitting it, because the Harry Wooton of those days was a big man in every sense of the word. Just the same, Gloucester was not his market, and as for his advice to 'find my own markets', that was a practical impossibility. There were Harry Wootons and Lichfield Georges in every market, all harbouring the misconception that the deeds of the place were in their pockets. In fact, the very name cattle market was misleading because they weren't markets at all. They were battlefields, and as for his first bit, that was the complete opposite of the truth. I was more than content with buying a handful or so each week and what's more, always most careful to watch my P's and Q's while doing it. It was Harry Wooton who was making off with the lion's share, five or six loads every Saturday, and money-spinners every one. The man was making a bomb and I couldn't have cared less.

There are those who believe that market prices are manipulated by a privileged handful of tough men, mainly through devices known as price rings, and although this could well be true of some trades, and in some countries, in thirty years in the meat trade, I've never come across anything of that nature. For one thing, there's far too much envy and jealousy, and for another, the modern English farmer would never stand for it. It all dates back to the old days when things were vastly different. When cattle had to be walked to market, the farmers were more or less at the mercy of the local villains, but all that went out, even before the draught horses. Nowadays, and that applies equally to the period I'm describing, cattle are transported cheaply and speedily hundreds of miles, and the merest suspicion of a price ring would be enough to see a market with no cattle to sell. Just the same, human nature being what it is, there were, and still are, subtleties that are unavoidable, and within limits, perfectly legitimate.

Every market has its school of top-dogs, and the only way to gain admittance is by perseverance. My entry into Gloucester Market has been set down exactly as it happened, and if it seems a fairly simple process, it's only because I was extremely fortunate and have always been aware of it. Partly on account of my dad's good name and reputation, and certainly with the help of Harry Wooton (which I still acknowledge in spite of everything), the barriers were lowered artificially, and without such help, the story would have been very different. What usually happened was that the established school only looked after itself and its members, and any outsider would find that, however carefully he trod, one or another of the regulars would chase him to the bitter end.

The only thing to do when faced with such antics is to take them all on. Grasping the nettle I believe it's called, and take it from me, it's possible to be stung to death doing it. Furthermore, if the newcomer was not sufficiently organised at the selling end, he was unable to dish up this sort of medicine in strong enough doses and likely to go on knocking at the door forever. Also he must know his business, at least as well as the best of them, otherwise there was a strong possibility of merely making a fool of himself and paying a lot of money for the privilege. In short, the only things the men who matter have any respect for are knowledge of cattle and strength of character, and it can take months to convince them. Once accepted, life becomes considerably easier. The hard-heads will laugh at your jokes, smoke your cigarettes, and keep their peace when you make your effort; although there's nothing permanent about it because there are still the niceties to be observed.

To bid on one of the school is always dangerous. At best, it can cause grumbles to rumble and eyes to flash, and at worst, the war could break out all over again. Greed should remain totally unnoticeable, and even when genuinely desperate for cattle, the plate can only be pushed up so far, and then with apologies. Then, left till last, is the most challenging aspect. In order not to be guilty of upsetting the toughies by bidding on them, one must be lightening quick off the mark. With the first bid down to you, anyone else in the market is forced to bid second. In which case, it is your eyes that do the flashing and your bid on top becomes perfectly legitimate. All sales then, according to the etiquette I've described (and always practised), are in effect Dutch auctions. The first bid is more important than the last, and rather than price rings, that keep values artificially low, bids are in the main 'lock-outs', that tend to keep prices high.

But now alas, with Harry Wooton's wrath about to descend, the situation changes completely, and so do all the rules. The wings I had so proudly thought I'd won had merely been lent. Harry had now claimed them back and if he had his way, even if I managed to keep them, I wouldn't have a shirt to pin them to. I looked forward to the next Saturday with very definite apprehension. I'll even admit to some fear and trepidation, but there was one thing for absolutely certain – there was no possibility of my not going.

War Clouds

•

Another of my dad's peculiarities was that, although he hated trouble and was highly skilled in its avoidance, when it was inevitable, he seemed to take it in his stride and almost enjoy it. He'd seen this crash with Harry Wooton coming ages ago as I knew only too well. According to his theory, all I'd got to do was start making money out of Gloucester and the fight was on – the thing to do now was to win it.

'Don't try to make him lose money,' was the first rule and also the main theme of the Friday evening tactical sermon. 'Everybody does that, and usually finish up in Carey Street. Take him up to the last quid or so, then drop out. That's the way to bugger Harry Wooton about. If he earns a few bob so much the better. He's not used to working for shillings. He'll soon get fed up with that caper.'

All good sense I had to admit, and sounded quite easy on the Friday, with my dad's assurance as thick as his cigar smoke, whichever way I looked. Now it was the morning after. I'd been standing in the cattle ring at Gloucester for nearly five minutes, waiting for the bell to go and although it was early autumn, I felt cold inside and out. The place was crammed with cattle and I should have been looking forward to a prof-itable day's work – in normal times that is. As it was, all I could think about was David and Goliath although, to be sure, if I'd paid a bit more attention to my scripture lessons there'd have been comfort to be gained even from that. With a minute or so to go, the gang started drifting into the ring laughing and yelling like circus clowns until the ring was full, and the bell went. I hadn't actually seen Harry Wooton, but a tingling sensa-tion at the back of the neck told me he wasn't far away, and it was right.

First, I had to establish that the situation was actually as serious as I thought. A volatile man like Harry Wooton might have been worked up about something or other the week before and had time to cool off by now, which would have suited me fine. I came to Gloucester to be a happy cattle buyer not a bloody-nosed hero and besides, while it's a pos-itive pleasure to fall foul of riff-raff the likes of Lichfield George, the really dangerous men usually have more than one side to their personality, which is probably what makes them dangerous.

Harry Wooton had been a background figure since my boyhood, a bit of a rogue admittedly, but just the same, I liked the man. It was Harry himself who first suggested to my dad that I should find my own market. 'Let him have a go Jake. You don't want to keep the lad hanging on to your shirt-tail forever, do you?' And another thing, my dad was so sure of his analysis of Harry Wooton, it would have been grand to prove him wrong for once.

It didn't take long.

For a comparative newcomer to start getting busy right at the beginning of a sale was to ask for trouble. Feeling your feet they call it, and my normal practice was to let the first couple of dozen go through without trying. Truth to tell, it took me that long to warm up anyway. But that, as I say, was my normal way. On that particular Saturday the situation was anything but normal. The very first cow to enter the ring was roughly similar to the one that started it all, gradeable without doubt and weighing about ten and a half-hundredweight. I stood in the centre of the ring where everyone could see and called out, 'Twenty-two Pounds.'

'Twenty-five.'

Harry Wooton stood there, also in full view, cool and calm and looking like the side of a house.

'Twenty-six.'

'Twenty-eight.'

'Twenty-nine.'

'Have it all Gaffer – thirty pounds.' That was Harry. I'd had enough and I stopped. The hammer came down with a crack and the auctioneer said, '…Wooton.'

'Look out chaps.' That was Frank. 'There's a war on,' and he didn't know just how right he was.

One thing about it, I'd started off right. Harry Wooton had bought his first cow under Shutkever rules – if I had estimated the weight correctly he was not going to get very fat out of that one. All that was required to make it a highly successful day, was to keep it up till the end of the sale and drive home with an empty lorry – which only goes to show just how daft cattlemen's wars were. For the next half hour it continued very well. We had four fast and furious tussles, and each time, I managed to pull out and leave Harry with what I considered were harmless purchases. Harry then resorted to psychological warfare. Having bought two cows one after the other, with me chasing him all the way, he turned full face and said, 'If that's the best you can do lad, you might as well have stayed at home.' All in a very friendly and matter-of-fact tone.

I'd actually calmed down enough by then to find the right answer.

'Don't want to be too hard on you Harry, after all, it is your market.' This pleased the glee club no end and must have hit the spot because he didn't try that one again for the rest of the day. I only knew one trick, which I couldn't resist trying, although to be sure, the gang ruined it for me every time. By stopping bidding a few pounds before the real value, it's possible to create the impression that you had misjudged the value of the animal and allowed your opponent to make off with something. But just before the hammer comes down, start the bidding again and carry on like fury right to the bitter end. It's a teasing manoeuvre and a very old soldier indeed; slow-timing, it's called. The trouble was that the mob wouldn't wear it and always the cry went up.

'...Come on young Jake, you're missing your turn...' or else,

'...I thought you two were having the bags on?' or yet again,

'...that's it chaps, the war's over, we can all go home...'

There was no doubt about it, the glee club were having a grand time and small wonder. Harry Wooton was too strong for most of them, and if they weren't actually frightened of him, 'over-awed' would about cover it. In consequence, they had stood and watched him taking more than his share out of Gloucester for years, so just to see someone give him a run for his money, even a novice like me, who was probably on the brink of annihilation, was better than going to the pictures (or wherever it was they went). Better yet. With Harry devoting all his efforts on mauling me about, they could help themselves and with my full blessing. For a greedy bugger like Harry Wooton to have to stand and watch others winning bargains when he couldn't (if I did the job right), was undoubtedly the biggest punishment of all.

Unfortunately there was one sphere in which Harry Wooton had me badly out-gunned, and to make matters worse we both knew of it. The bulk of the cattle at Gloucester were respectable and gradeable and with them, apart from mis-judgments and miscalculations, danger was minimal. At worst, I might take things too far and finish up with one or two that earn nothing (or God forbid lose a bit), or perhaps not go far enough and allow Harry to earn more than the desired few bob. Even the very poor specimens were no problem because we still had our knacker connection although, to be sure, our £15 limit was a bit cramping, to say the least. It was with the ones in between that the real danger lurked, the 'border-liners', and, as I say, Harry Wooton was well aware of it. Every time one of those skinny lizzies came ambling into the ring he would set up the bidding and dare me to chase him. It was like playing Russian roulette with knacker cows, fifty times every Saturday and every bit as dangerous. Harry Wooton was an agent for a large knacker meat establishment there in Gloucester and his limit was a good £10 better than mine; which was something else we both knew and, of course, nobody's luck lasts forever. Before the day was out, I had managed to land myself with three really bad old dolls, each one costing over twenty pounds, and without the slightest idea of what I was going to do with them.

It was, however, at the other end of the scale that the master plan really started to go adrift, because when the best cattle began to enter the ring, I found myself buying, and in alarming quantities by my standards. I stuck to the rules as before, but it didn't seem to be working and by midday, I had three lorry loads down to me, with plenty more still to come and getting a bit worried about it. The trouble was that they didn't go to the limit and in several cases were some way below it, so that a most terrible possibility darkened the horizon. Could it be that I was over-estimating the weights and thereby setting the limits too high? Not impossible by any means; my normal judgements always erred on the high side. I was big-eyed, as my dad used to say. When I checked in my book and found thirty-four in it, I decided it was time to 'pull my horns in' a bit before I got swamped completely. I looked harder, took more care and allowed an extra pound or so, but it made no difference because I still went on buying.

One heifer I remember quite clearly. I 'called her' eight-hundred-weight, and whichever way I looked, couldn't make her any less, so at £6 per hundredweight, she was worth £48. I bought her for £42 with Harry Wooton running her all the way and dropping out at £41.75. By the end of the day, after fighting it out with Harry Wooton from first to last, I was whacked. I don't how many he finished up with and I don't really care, although I saw several pens full of cattle bearing his mark. I bought six lorry-loads – fifty-two cattle – which was more than I usually bought in a month, and I'd left home that morning intending to buy nothing at all. Mind blowing, that's what it was, the stuff of which nervous breakdowns are made.

The following morning I was still in a daze. Even my dad was strangely quiet on the way over to my place for the inspection ritual. He knew I'd managed to get myself loaded up to the eyebrows, because I'd already handed him my auctioneer's ticket, and normally he'd have jumped the gun and started telling me where I'd gone wrong, even before seeing the result (and it was amazing how often he was right). That day he didn't, and we'd walked round that field full of new arrivals with hardly a word spoken since leaving home. He gave those cattle a thorough vetting, and although the briefest of glances was normally enough, that day he took his time about it until I thought he was never going to finish. He then rubbed his nose between finger and thumb, a gesture reserved only for the most complicated of decisions.

'There's something wrong here Harry.' (Even that was unusual because he never called me anything other than 'lad', unless he was annoyed, when it became 'my Lad'.) 'I don't know what to make of it and that's a fact.' It was one of those rare occasions we were in complete agreement – I couldn't understand it either. He took another little tour round the field, occasionally glancing from the ticket to the cattle and back, and then came the verdict – very calm and very precise. 'There's five or six heifers here that are cheap. That little bugger over there will earn you a tenner, and there must be fifteen or twenty that'll earn three or four apiece. Mind you, the cows aren't much cop. You'll have to do the best you can with them on Monday.' Slowly and deliberately he then jabbed a finger at each of my three old dolls in turn, 'and what do you think you're going to do with those three varmints?' It was what they call a very good question.

'I couldn't help them I'm afraid, Wooton blew first.'

'Take 'em on to Lichfield tomorrow, I'll find a home for 'em somehow.' He was a funny chap, my dad. I was expecting a right roasting over those three.

'Was Wooton in the ring all day?'

'From start to finish.'

'And he didn't try to call it off?'

'Not a bit of it. If anything, he got rougher. If it had gone on much longer, I think he'd have blown up.'

'Well, all I can say is you're lucky lad. He's a bigger mug than I thought he was.'

For the second time in less than an hour I found myself in complete agreement. I was indeed lucky. Had I been up against a cattle judge of my dad's calibre the story would have been vastly different – Louis Shutkever would have made mincemeat out of me.

Just the same, the thing must be seen in its correct perspective. It was the back-end of the year when cattle were cheap and plentiful every-where, and Harry Wooton could have been bunged-up with cattle to the extent that he had no option. It happened to all of us from time to time. He could also have been playing the same game I had intended. Loading the other chap up; although, if that was the case, he'd not made too good a job of it. Apart from the three old cows he hadn't loaded me up at all and if that was his method of getting me in trouble, I hoped he'd do it every week. Harry Wooton was rough, tough, and making a lot of money, and where the lower category of cow was concerned, he could always give me a thrashing, but on the strength of that first day I knew he wasn't the judge of cattle he should have been. I no longer saw the situation as desperate, or anything like it, and have never been frightened of Harry Wooton or anyone else since. I also discovered that size and reputation were not necessarily the advantage they seemed, and, in fact, could prove themselves the very reverse. Being the undisputed master of the low-category cow business was a title that needed to be defended, leaving Harry Wooton compelled to take such animals right to the top limit. Whereas I could drop out anywhere near the last pound or so and consider the job well done.

Then there was the numbers game, which also worked against him. The few cattle I needed could be found almost anywhere, whereas he was grading something like two hundred cattle every week and, no doubt, depended on Gloucester for a fair percentage of them. So, one way and another, I summed the situation up as not discouraging and without actually looking forward to the next Saturday, I certainly wasn't dreading it. For what it's worth the three old cows went through the ring at Lichfield and lost five pounds between them – I was more than satisfied.

That was to be the pattern for a long time to come. A long, testing slog, more of a siege than a battle, and might have killed me off but for two important developments in the early stages. From amongst the gang, I found two strong allies, as well as a host of well-wishers who, while not so important, were very welcome just the same. The first was Frank, who saw fit to announce whose side he was on in no uncertain manner.

'Harry Wooton, you ought to be ashamed of yourself,' and this from the centre of the ring and in a loud voice that all but stopped the sale. 'This young chap wore khaki for you. He comes here to try to earn a few quid and you feel obliged to set about him.'

I hadn't complained to Frank or to anyone else; it was quite spontaneous and took me by surprise – although it was in keeping with Frank's general attitude to the job. When it came to fun and games he was up there with the rest and, often as not, the ringleader, but only to a point. Real flashes of temper or anything likely to build up into serious confrontations were not to his liking. Frank had the brains to see that cattlemen's wars were no different to any other wars – no one won them, so his '…steady now chaps there's plenty for everyone…' was quite often all that was required to cool things down. His verbal encouragement was very welcome, but it didn't end there. Later that day, he came over with some sound advice and also an offer of practical assistance.

'Don't let Harry Wooton throw you lad. He thinks he's clever but he doesn't know it all.' He then looked me straight in the eye and winked. 'You don't need me to tell you that do you? You've just pinched a bullock right under his nose.' It was true. I had, although until then, I hadn't realised anyone else had noticed. Frank then came in close.

'Watch him with the cows. He's trying everything to drop a cripple or two on your toe. In any case, if you want a load or two for the 'M' job, all you've got to do is give me a ring any evening. I'll get you as many as you want and if they don't earn you money, you needn't pay me for 'em.'

What's more, he did. I had several loads from him over the next few months, all with the original auction tickets still on, and accompanied by the sale bills to show there was no jiggery-pokery. They earned me profit and I paid Frank a commission, although he didn't want it and I had to insist. He was by no means wealthy; in fact, several years later, I received the sad news that he had gone bankrupt.

The other offer of help was a different matter entirely and came from a big, hard-headed and ugly man who was not really a friend at all, although he probably saved my bacon just the same. There was a knacker-erman's war at Gloucester, just like the one at Banbury, fiercer even, because the two principals rubbed noses right there in the market every Saturday. So with Harry Wooton firmly entrenched with the one, it called for no great feat of diplomacy on my behalf to become enrolled with the other.

Unfortunately for me, at that particular time, the Gloucester knacker-men's war was enjoying a cold period. Noses were getting rubbed rather than broken, and my side, at least, were anxious to do nothing that could be termed provocative, or rather I should say, not get caught doing it. A spot of crafty subterfuge was called for, a smuggling operation in fact. Any 'dead-beats' Harry Wooton managed to land me with were loaded onto my lorry and driven round to a car park on the other side of the town. There I would rendezvous with my new-found ally for the transfer. The two lorries backed up close like copulating insects.

There's no knowing just how we got rumbled, although it was always a risky business; something like playing with matches in a fireworks factory and couldn't be expected to continue indefinitely. Harry Wooton had spies everywhere. For the price of a pint there were those among the Gloucester drovers who would cheerfully have sold their own mothers. I had two of my own, keeping a watchful eye on the lorries unloading just in case Harry tried to bring a few cows to 'pitch' into me. What matters was that we were rumbled, the predictable outcome being the lid flew off the Gloucester knackermen's war and those two gentlemen began to waste another small fortune. With them knocking spots off each other, I no longer had a knacker cow problem, and if I didn't feel too badly about it, that was only because they seemed to be enjoying themselves so much.

The war with Harry Wooton slowed down the progress I had been making – I'll admit to that – and if his object had been to disappoint my tax-man for a year or so, he was probably successful there as well. But that was all. It only needed to look back to the time prior to the confrontation he inspired, and compare the loads of bargains he'd been making off with then, to what he had to be content with after, to know that I hurt him badly, and if that sounds conceited, it's also true. But I like to think that I won the battle for a different reason altogether.

The school at Gloucester were kind to me from the start, and I was always aware of it. I was a boy in a man's world and they treated me as such, not taking me too seriously, but not bullying me either, but after I fell foul of Harry Wooton there was a subtle change. Without becoming a king – or even a prince – I was allowed to take a man's share out of the cattle at Gloucester Market and still retain the blessing of most of them. In a sentence, the day Harry Wooton decided to sling me out of Gloucester, was the day I lost my amateur status.

Harry Wooton, old son – I owe you!

For what it's worth, the Wooton-Shutkever war went on for years. In fact, the armistice has never been declared. What has happened is that the meat trade has changed completely since those days and now I see little of him and don't much mind that.

Banbury

•

Banbury Market, even in those days, was by far our biggest market and our busiest day; today it is a huge affair and still growing. As well as an acre or so of sheep pens, and a colossal enclosed pig marketing hall, there are three cattle rings, all enclosed and air-conditioned, seated accommodation for the buyers, and even vending machines. The Principal was a frail old Scotsman, never an auctioneer himself and, in any case, way beyond the age of retirement by the time I met him. My dad always held him in great esteem. Probably because he had the foresight to embark on a grandiose expansion scheme when farming in general had long been in the doldrums. My dad always respected gutsy people. The chief auctioneer was the first and last of his breed I ever came across, with that high-speed, sing-song American style they've since set to music, and it was a full six months before I could decipher a single word he was warbling. There were still the inevitable cat-calls and slogans, but also an atmosphere of seriousness. The few Gloucester men who attended occasionally found fit to reserve their frolics for Saturday. At Banbury, decorum was the order of the day, yet there were tricks and tricky characters, just like anywhere else, the difference being that the scale was bigger to match the place itself.

The fat cattle sale started at twelve o'clock, the animals going through the ring at a spanking two or three a minute until about six o'clock, depending on the season. On my first day, I sat on the wooden, amphitheatre-type steps trying to follow the proceedings and booking down the cattle as my dad bought them. After about an hour a heavily-built man, somewhat older than my dad, came up and sat next to him and a conversation struck up from the start. They talked about racing, the cattle business, a few reminiscences of the old days, and appeared to have lost all interest in the sale whatsoever. This struck me as very odd. My dad was never a gossiper and if I was any judge at all, the other chap was of the same mould, yet there they sat for perhaps half-an-hour, letting the day slip by, like a couple of fishwives. Eventually he creaked into a standing position and made off – I felt compelled to investigate.

'What was that all about?'

'That was Spen Houlton.'

'Who's he?'

'He's a cute bugger he is, the biggest supplier in the whole market. Like a fly in a bottle is Spen.'

'Didn't seem over-busy to me.'

'That's because you don't know – he's just shown over two hundred cattle, and sold most of 'em.'

'When?'

'Now, you've just sat and watched him do it.' He then explained Spen Houlton's technique and, although it sounded simple enough, I didn't realise the full implication until I watched a repeat performance the following Thursday. Perhaps I should mention that vendors were always at liberty to place a reserve on their cattle and until that price is reached the auctioneer would 'run it up' himself. If, after the reserve was reached there was no genuine bid, the animal would be declared 'not sold' and return from whence it came – or perhaps be sold privately afterwards. Spen Houlton, however, had a method all his own.

He sat where the auctioneer could see him, with his walking stick hooked over his shoulder, and while it remained there the bids kept rising. Once Spen Houlton was satisfied with the price, the stick was removed and the auctioneer was free to sell.

The remarkable thing was that Houlton carried it all in his head, and without recourse to any written information, knew the cost of every one of his cattle and when to remove his stick – and they were different cattle every week. Furthermore, he still had the capacity to carry on a conversation normal enough to deceive me at least. I have since come to realise that this – part gift and part knack – is not uncommon in the cattle business. My dad could remember cattle and prices for years, but I've never seen it done so casually, or on so big a scale, and certainly not at Banbury Market speed. Spen Houlton was a cute bugger all right, and yet, not many weeks later, I managed to outflank the pair of them and learn something of human nature at the same time.

I had learned the cow-heifer trick by then, and the searches had already become standard practice. My dad had introduced me to Houlton's drover and an understanding was reached whereby he would point out the pens that held Houlton's cattle. This was simply to save me the trouble of fighting my way through a hundred or more cattle when there was no danger of stealing anything. Although they were good pals, my dad rarely tried to buy Houlton's cattle. Spen was too cute and my dad looked for easier prey. But one day I made a mistake and searched through two of Houlton's pens by accident. In amongst them was a large, white, fairly ancient-looking cow that quite unbelievably still had one calf tooth left. The drover saw me and pointed out that I had strayed onto Holy Ground, so I didn't even bother to include her on my list.

The sale got underway and we were eventually joined by friend Spen for the weekly chatter, when, in came that white cow. I was still very much of a novice. We have gone back to a time when I'd never even dreamed of buying in auction, and certainly not at Banbury. However, when the price reached £36 and I saw the stick removed from Spen's shoulder, even I could calculate that something was amiss – she was every bit of twelve-hundredweight and worth something over £50. I had a moment of sheer panic. I wasn't sure of anything at all. I thought the auctioneer was singing '36...36...36,' but it could quite easily have been '56...56...56,' and it could have been a different cow. Also, it wasn't on the list and, in any case, my dad would not have thought to look because he knew already that those pens were never searched. There was no time to tell him either and in any case he'd never have believed it – I couldn't believe it myself. And all the time, the precious seconds were ticking by. At any moment that little hammer would come thundering down and it would be gone forever. I simply could not let that happen. I waved my outside hand, the one away from both Houlton and my dad, and winked like mad at the auctioneer, who possibly hadn't even got a genuine bid. He spotted me at once.

Bang went the hammer. 'Shutkever,' he shouted.

My dad sat up as though he'd been stung. I never knew him to move faster, and Spen looked as bewildered as I felt. Then, horror of horrors, my dad was already trying to attract the auctioneer's attention to dispute the bid. I had to do something.

'It was me – it's a cow-heifer.' My dad stared at me like I was a green man from Mars. I think that was the first time I noticed his eyes were tawny brown: 'You sure?'

'I was then – I'm not so sure now.' It was right, I wasn't.

They looked at each other, completely dumbfounded and expressionless at the same time. It was a good job I watched the performance because I was never to see either of them so confused again. My dad recovered first.

'Slip round to my pen and have another look,' a needless command if ever there was one. Once I'd got my breath back, nothing could have stopped me.

It was there all right, a gleaming little calf tooth, and firm as a rock.

And they thought it very funny. One had just been robbed of a cool fifteen pounds and the other was party to it, and those two hard-heads laughed like drains. It's passed on to become a very small part of the folk-lore. For years afterwards I would meet up with Spen Houlton while touring round the Banbury pens, to be solemnly shaken by the hand and asked, 'What are you up to Young Shutkever – looking for another cow-heifer like the last one I sold you?'

I was baffled by another little mystery at Banbury in those early days. The last row of pens was reserved for store cattle that were sold after the fat cattle were finished. Store cattle at other markets were a normal mixture; Friesians, Herefords, Shorthorns, good, bad, and indifferent, but in that row, the animals were remarkably alike. They were good cattle, deep red Herefords, varying in age and size but with a similarity that even an unpractised eye like mine could not but notice. The second part of the puzzle was that although my dad bought and supplied quite substantial numbers of stores, he never gave that row as much as a look, his pre-market tour finishing where that row began. When I asked him why, my dad explained, so although there was nothing wildly exciting about it, I think it worth including as just one more aspect of the complicated business I was being pitch-forked into.

The cattle in question came, if I remember correctly, mainly from Ireland, and were the property of an old-established, old-fashioned and quite respectable family of cattle dealers. But, like Spen Houlton, they had methods of their own which were more than likely adopted from their Irish counterparts, because the whole system smacked highly of the Celtic. They sent the cattle through the ring with a somewhat high reserve, and for those that got sold, it was well and good. The majority however would be 'bought in' (which means not sold) and returned to their pens. Then would come a haggle of their own, something in the style of the bygone street fair, the basis for negotiation being the slightly unnatural prices given out previously in the auction ring. There was nothing dishonest about it, except that any sales so made were not registered through the office and the sale yard received no commission. The practice was frowned on, rather than objected to, mainly because the family were quite respectable, had long-standing association with Banbury Market, and I believe them to have been substantial shareholders in the company. There was something of the old pals' act about the whole thing. Anyway, having had the set-up explained, I saw quite easily why my dad looked elsewhere for his stores.

Staying on the subject of store cattle, there was yet another character at Banbury I think well worth a mention, an amazing old chap. He was a white haired, but wiry man, in his sixties who always wore riding breeches, hacking jacket, and cloth-cap; work-a-day rather than smart. With his piercing blue eyes and accent that would melt butter, he was almost too Irish to be true. And his business methods were more Irish even than that.

Paddy was a busy man, always to be found striding down the alleys, stooping to look between the rails, pushing his cap to the back of his head the better to mop up perspiration from a red forehead, in a massive show of concentration. Then he would straighten up, change direction and march back the way he had come, all the time darting sharp-eyed glances this way and that, obviously looking for someone. A really busy man was Paddy and no mistake. Next, he could be seen with a farmer, standing very close-up and whispering conspiratorially, hands and stick pointing agitatedly in all directions, until he would lead off down the alley, still talking, and glancing back over his shoulder to ensure he was being followed. Paddy was selling cattle. Over the years he must have sold hundreds, and there's nothing remarkable about that; dozens of men were doing precisely the same in Banbury every Thursday. No, the amazing bit was that the cattle he was selling weren't his own and, quite often, he didn't know whose they were. And before the wrath of all Ireland descends on my head, let me say here and now, that to the best of my belief, he was an honest man. There might be more of his kind scattered about, although I never encountered any, so to me at least, old Paddy was unique.

He sold his cattle first, then went on a frantic search of the market to find the owner and try to buy them afterwards, at all times with three strings to his bow. If he sold high enough and bought low enough, he made a handsome profit with no expenses; it's the sort of thing that happens on the stockmarket every day of the week. If he didn't do quite so well, and only broke even, all was not lost because there was always commission to be squeezed from either or both ends. Occasionally, of course, a scheme so precarious had to come unstuck. He couldn't find the owner or else the man wouldn't sell. Then he simply went back to his buyer and with beautifully-worded apologies, declared the deal null and void, after which he looked for some more cattle and another likely customer, and the whole thing started up again. He never actually paid for anything, for the simple reason that old Paddy never had two halfpennies to rub together.

The other one I can't leave out was Jesse Smith; a small, thick-lipped and ugly man in a wide-brimmed hat. Jesse was a gypsy horse trader. A real one, not to be confused with today's imitations, and it's a fairly safe bet there weren't many more like him. Where he or his cattle came from I never found out, but quite frequently, he brought some to Banbury and was never happier then when trying to sell them to my dad. There was a natural affinity between those two because my dad always liked the clever eccentric. They had to be clever, mind, he had absolutely no time for cranks or barmpots. Jesse was not only a real gypsy, but he spoke in a gypsy way, '… coma Jake, buyem offa me,' and, as with the auctioneer, it was some time before I could understand. So what with my dad and Jesse Smith together smashing chunks off the English language, it was always something of a linguist's nightmare. In this way, they argued for shillings and although it often led to cattle changing hands I'm absolutely certain that for them both, the fight was worth more than the prize. The tale I want to tell about this gypsy is my dad's, rather than my own, because it all happened years before my time.

Jesse turned up at Banbury with a large envelope, the contents of which were offered for my dad to inspect. It was a builder's plan for a pair of semi-detached houses; not really Shutkever's sphere, although what was under discussion was the estimate rather than the technicalities, and here he could voice an opinion. As it happened, a few similar dwellings had been built on this farm around that time, so current building costs were not unknown In any case, to Jesse Smith, Jake was an authority on anything to do with money. At about four-hundred pound a pair, my dad could find little to complain about and said as much. Smith went away content, although it didn't end there. He approached his builder again and asked for another quote, but this time for a dozen pairs of houses rather than the one; the transaction eventually finalised at under three hundred pound a pair. When the houses were finished, little Gypsy Smith, who haggled for shillings, gave the whole lot to his daughter for a wedding present. They stand there today, on the right hand side of the road, just outside Banbury on the way to Birmingham, a probable one & a half-million pounds worth of real estate, and my dad never passed them without reminding me of the story.

To me, Thursday still means Banbury Market. I can't think of the one without the other. It was the big day of the week for many long years, although not my dad's favourite market, any more than it was mine. Now I'm not saying that his ghost lives there, because I really don't believe in such things, and he's been gone these many years, yet on the rare visits I still make there I feel closer to my dad at Banbury than anywhere else.

End of an Era

•

The big change we were all expecting arrived in the spring of 1954. Not only meat rationing, but the entire system I have tried to set down in this book was to be wound up in July; collecting centres, graders, cow-heifers (and the searches for them). The whole shooting-match. A sprinkling of white coats among the market spectators was perhaps the first practical sign that, after fourteen years of artificial trading, the meat trade was shortly to be handed back to its rightful owners. There was much excited talk and knowledgeable speculation, deeply secret plans were being hatched, and there was a tension in the air, that I liken to a bow-string being pulled, with the arrow pointing in several unknown directions. The real attitude to the coming eruption was best summed-up in one short sentence by Gloucester Frank.

'Make the most of it chaps,' he yelled, embarrassing a couple of white-coated spectators by pointing them out with his long stick. 'They're coming back.'

I've never been able to decide whether or not I was lucky, regarding that fourteen-year period of meat control and rationing, although, to be sure, I was better placed than a good many others. At least the time had been put to good use. For some years I'd been judging weights, buying in auction, and earning a modest living out of it. Whereas in the case of many who could be termed my contemporaries, the situation was vastly different and, in my view, inferior. They had taken jobs with the Ministry of Food and far from being cattlemen or meat men of any description, they had become clerks and weigh-men and hardly knew one end of a bullock from the other. However, there I was, twenty-seven years of age, son of a well-known wholesaler, and had yet to sell my first piece of meat or, for that matter, set foot in my first real abattoir. I had been robbed, no doubt about it, but not nearly as badly as some and, in my case, there was also a very important compensatory factor. Many of the pre-war master-men had died or retired with no possibility of training replacements; perhaps the main reason why many old-established Birmingham meat firms never did re-open their doors. Harry Shutkever had a secret weapon, a veritable block-buster, because at that most crucial of times, my dad was a mere stripling of fifty-six – and with all his buttons on, I can assure you. Who better then to pick up the meat business from where it was left back in 1940 than Shutkever and Son. Yet for all this, my dad's view had suffered a slight change quite recently, or so it seemed to me.

The difference between us was that he knew both sides of the coin and I didn't. After years of saying quite categorically that he was itching to get back to work, with the prospect just around the corner, he was having second thoughts. Suddenly he saw the meat trade proper as nothing less than slavery. A half-past-five start to a long hard day, six days a week, hides and by-products to be disposed of every day, bills to send out and cash to collect. All of these needed a large staff of both office and trade workers when, for these many years, we'd been earning a happy living with just ourselves and a couple of farmhands. Also, he had gained some weight, too much in fact; the Ministry of Food's system had softened him up, God help us, and I should have been warned by that. But I had my own reasons for wanting to see the back of the Ministry of Food system, and the sooner the better.

The Lichfield George's and the Harry Wooton's had had things their way far too long. It was high time they moved over to make room for the real meat trade. That was what I was looking forward to. Cattle had become valued at whatever the graders could be kidded into offering, and without wishing to put too fine a point on it, there were those who had become rather too well-organised at that particular caper – open to abuse was how I described it, I think. All that was going. In the new order of things, cattle would be worth what a meat-salesman could sell the meat for; no tricks, no nonsense, and no preferential treatment. That's what I was looking forward to. Equal terms for a change.

Harry Wooton had been mauling me about at Gloucester for something like three years by then. I think I was giving at least as good as I got and in any case, I'd become used to it and it didn't bother me all that much. Just the same, I am not, and have never been a masochist, and from my viewpoint, the old system was about to depart and take Harry Wooton's big stick along with it; can't be bad I thought – worth getting up at half-past five for! It had also occurred to me that if everybody else had to be up at the crack, and selling meat in fair competition before setting out to the cattle markets, there was just a chance they wouldn't be quite so reckless with their money when they arrived there.

I can now say, and with hindsight, that some of those thoughts were perhaps a little naïve, over-optimistic in fact. Although no more than could be expected from someone who'd never seen the real meat trade. In one aspect, however, they hit the nail fair and square. From July 1954 onwards, Harry Wooton and all his merry men had to make do with sticks no bigger than anyone else's and, in some cases, not even as big. Some of them had become almost unrecognizable.

As it never occurred to me, at the time, that perhaps I might one day attempt to chronicle the meat trade, I have no notes with which to assist a fairly mediocre memory. I do remember the struggle to find slaughtermen and my dad's way of getting them. He had an uncanny way of seeing and countering future obstacles, and had always kept in touch with Percy Tricklebank, an old slaughterman whose several sons were skilled operators, plying their trade in various abattoirs scattered about the Midlands. I also remember the completely inadequate office set-up that collapsed in a heap on the first Friday; the shortage of humpers to carry the meat and the problems we had with the ones we'd got, and all the near catastrophes after the change, and will deal with them in due course. But the weeks immediately prior to it have become blurred, although I did discover the very real reason for my dad's sudden lack of enthusiasm. His cleverness was all to do with basics. No amount of trade problems could throw him. In fact, the more difficult the problem, the easier he seemed to find the remedy. It was office work and the day-to-day organisation of that side of the business that upset him. He just couldn't be bothered with it and would sit there getting more or more worked up and edgy as Hell. Office systems are a mystery to me as well, and I went to several schools.

One thing, however, I do remember.

Right from the beginning I have been anxious to point out my dad's absolute determination that I be independent. It was almost a religion with him and long were the discussions and schemes we devised to bring it about.

By the first week, in July 1954, we had two farms full of cattle between the pair of us and were making plans for the immediate future. At the time, there was something of a stampede to the collecting centres to get rid of as many as possible while the dear old Ministry of Food was still in business. My dad didn't see it quite like that. He foresaw meat going up in price, both suddenly and steeply, so while we did get rid of the cows, all the best cattle were kept and even added to, until we could hold no more. When the end came, we had two-hundred and forty cattle on the two farms; all paid for, some by him and some by me. I had kept my own books, paid my own income tax, and carefully recorded all my livestock at cost, all the way through. At that precise time, I owned one-hundred and eight cattle that owed me £72 apiece.

Yes. Here it comes, stranger than any fiction is this.

From the first day of our return to real wholesale butchering, the whole caboodle was shot together into one autonomous mass. My carefully kept stock book went the same way as my transport records of earlier vintage. I kept them both for years and it did me not a scrap of good.

We were now Shutkever and Son – once and for all, and that's the way it stayed.

Percy Tricklebank

•

July 1954 was one of the rare times when my dad put his neck on the block and believe me, he didn't enjoy the experience any more than I enjoyed watching it. It was dead against his nature. He always liked to keep the whip in his own hands, and Old Percy Tricklebank's perform-ance in the last hour or so hadn't helped matters. It was as much as Percy could manage to escort us the length of his driveway back to the car, and when he leaned in through the window his breath sent me reeling.

'I've told you not to worry, haven't I?'

The voice was old and dry as parchment, and the hand that came into the car to emphasise the words, shook bits of Woodbine ash all over the carpet.

'I saw the Big 'Un yesterday. He's got the men exactly as we said and if you go to town at eleven o'clock on Sunday morning, you'll see 'em for yourself.'

My dad nodded and tried to look satisfied but didn't make too good a job of it; I wasn't convinced, for one. As the engine started, Old Percy stuck his grizzled head inside and breathed a last word all over us.

'Don't worry Mr Shutkever, they'll be there, and no rubbing-rags. Good butchers every one of 'em.'

We'd sat in his cottage for upwards of an hour and heard him make the same assertion at least a dozen times. All in the same agitated manner, and all with the same negative effect, especially on my dad. I've already stated his attitude to drink – it was an excuse for failure, as well as a rea-son for it, yet there he was, only a few days away from what was probably the biggest crossroads of his life and the key to everything was in the hands of an old reprobate like Percy Tricklebank. And the only thing we knew for certain was that the man was well on the way to being drunk.

Percy Tricklebank was an old slaughterman from Derbyshire. Cloth cap, straw carrier bag, and everything, and although I'd known him for some years, I'd never got to know him well. It's not derogatory to say that his reputation as a womaniser (as well, incidentally, as a slaughterman) was already something of a legend because it was fully endorsed by Old Percy himself – 'you'll hear a lot of stories about me young man, and most of 'em are true.'

He'd been to the farm several times to take my dad on buying expeditions among his old pre-war mates, and occasionally he'd turn up at Stratford Market when, often as not, I'd give him a lift back to his cottage; an old, wooden, creosoted shack which, like Percy himself, had seen better days. He was always polite enough to address my dad by the formal 'Mr Shutkever', and thoughtful enough to insist I take some fruit or flowers home for my mother; an old-fashioned gesture from an old-fashioned cottage gardener. I only knew him as an old man. At the time of writing, he would have been in his seventies, slightly stooped and with little flesh on his old bones, but he was still six-feet tall and with a width of shoulder that plainly said he'd been a giant of a man in his time. By then, he'd been retired for some years but the old devil didn't like it very much and saw the return to normal meat trading as a chance to make a come-back.

For fourteen years skilled men had been leaving the meat trade, some killed in action, some spirited away by the lure of big money in war factories, and some simply retiring; fourteen years is a long time. Yet although often talked about, no serious attempt had been made to train replacements, not in our city anyway, and consequently skilled men, especially slaughtermen, had suddenly become scarcer than diamonds, which was where Old Percy Tricklebank came into the picture. My dad approached him and he didn't need asking twice '…all the men you want Mr Shutkever, and top butchers every one!'

Slaughtermen, incidentally, never refer to themselves or each other as 'slaughtermen', they are 'butchers' (not to be confused with men who run butcher shops who are called 'shop butchers'). The old reprobate had been so sure of himself and his ability to deliver that my dad had done nothing more about it, except to drop in on him from time to time, by way of a reminder. It was too late now anyway. Everything rested with Percy Tricklebank, and the state he was in was doing my dad's peace of mind no good whatever. Our tenancy agreement was signed, gun licence taken out, two hundred cattle bought and paid for, not to mention tools and blocks, overalls and wellingtons by the dozen, stationery by the packet, and so far, we hadn't so much as laid eyes on a slaughterman, let alone signed him up.

We had worried for nothing. At eleven o'clock the following Sunday, after an eight-mile drive into Birmingham, in a silence deep enough to steam up the windows, I stopped the car outside the city abattoir and there they were, a group of about twelve men. And in its centre, cloth cap perched almost on his long beak of a nose so that he had to peer out from under it, Mr Magoo himself – Percy Tricklebank had indeed delivered the goods.

There was one old chap I already knew, a small, white-haired veteran of similar vintage to Old Percy and not part of the bargain. Old Harry had worked for my dad before the war, both as a slaughterman and a cattle buyer and was there as of right. His son would also have been in the group had he not been killed at Anzio some ten years previously. Then there were a few clerical types comprising; one office clerk, one check-weighman and one scalesman, and that left Percy Tricklebank and his 'good butchers'. Apart from a few knackeryard cowboys here and there, I had never come face-to-face with any real live slaughtermen before in my life, and don't know just what I had expected to find, so perhaps I shouldn't have been surprised at all; but believe me I was, and agreeably at that.

Four of them were brothers. Percy Tricklebank's sons, dark-eyed, keen looking men who, although ranging in height from six-foot two (the Big 'Un) to about five-foot six (Young Stan), there was no mistaking where they came from – the Tricklebank stamp was on them all. They weren't clean and tidy. They were scrubbed and immaculate, in spotless white shirts, striped ties and navy blazers. If there'd been a few more they'd have looked like a university boat crew or a top-class football squad. I went to meet the men in sports jacket and flannels and found myself wishing I'd worn my best suit instead. There were three more slaughtermen, pals not family, who'd been roped in to make the number up, and while they might not have been quite as striking as the Tricklebanks, there was nothing wrong in the looks of them either.

The 'Big 'Un' was Bill Tricklebank, Big Bill to everybody except his dad, and I think he deserves a sentence or two to himself. He had earned something of a reputation as a wild man, mostly connected with fighting and drink, so that it was impossible to say which was cause and which effect. One thing was certain. When drunk, Big Bill was a very dangerous animal indeed, and once hit a man in a pub hard enough, not merely to go crashing through a plate glass window but to completely miss the pavement and finish up in the road. He'd also been to prison for something or other, although this should be judged in context because among the men in the meat trade, it's not the blemish that perhaps it should be. I knew all this already; Big Bill Tricklebank was as much a legend as was his dad, but that didn't stop him from impressing me the most. His handshake was the firmest, his look the most direct, and wild man or not, I liked him from the start.

We all stood chatting for a bit out there in the street, finalised the fact that we started work on the following Saturday (which sounds a cock-eyed day to start, but is in fact the only one) the group dispersed. My dad then led off into the market complex to show me our new place of business for the very first time.

Birmingham City Meat Market was surrounded by high, red-brick walls, with tall wooden gates topped with cast-iron spikes, stonework battlements and corner-pieces, all heavily carved and chiselled to a degree that told its own story. When it was built, superb craftsmen abounded and their artistry could be purchased cheaply enough for it to be lavished where few even bothered to look. Rather than a meat market or a market of any sort, if it resembled anything it was a Beau Geste fortress or perhaps a high-security gaol. It most certainly didn't belong where it was, not a stone's throw from the city centre, but there it had stood for a hundred years and was obviously built to last forever. There were those who found it an eyesore, and the trade it housed obnoxious – something to be hidden away from decent folk.– but I was never one of them. It was bitterly cold in winter, had uneven and somewhat slippery floors (to break the unwary leg), flaky paint-work on the overhead rails (to blind the unlucky eye) and a host of further drawbacks (including rats), but I thought it a grand old place, and despite my being a practising romantic, my reasons are all down-to-earth and practical. I'll say only that I have been in several modern abattoirs and meat sales halls since that time, some of them huge and costing millions (the one at Manchester covers a twenty-two acre site), but I've yet to see one better than the old Birmingham Market. The main asset was its height, forty-feet or more, which gave it a spaciousness of such degree that meat properly dressed and handled could be hung for several days, even in summer without need for refrigeration. There's also a thing called atmosphere, but I won't go into that.

What my dad showed me was a couple of areas perhaps seventy square-yards each, bordered only by the heavy cast-iron pillars of the main structure and nothing else; no back, front, or sides. There were about sixty such stalls in the market hall, equally divided between the fresh meat traders and the importers, and as pre-war tenants, we had been allocated those two. Overhead was a mass of steel rails, all bent and twisted into the most complicated of shapes, which my dad tried to explain (with little success) after which he walked me over to the slaughterhouse and described the system there (even less profitably). It's not that the thing was so devilishly difficult or that I was particularly thick. The place was empty, just a shell, and had about as much to see as Banbury Cattle Market on a Sunday. In any case my dad was probably the most un-mechanical of men and not the best of explainers either. He'd show me in the way he showed me everything else – with that bloody pitchfork of his.

But what I did see, and most welcome it was as well, was the tremendous change that had come over my dad himself, and all in the last hour. Percy Tricklebank hadn't let him down. He'd seen the men, obviously liked what he saw, and all at once it was the old Jake again; the glaring, staring, swearing, head-shaking old devil I'd got used to over the years. After the grey old man of the last couple of weeks, it was a positive pleasure to be blasphemed at by Jake, the cursing master I can tell you, and once he got going there was no stopping him. By the time we'd driven half-way home, he had given me a full week's work to be done that day and was thinking of something for Monday – a positive pleasure.

As I got to know Old Percy Tricklebank better, I came to realise that my estimation of the situation that day at his cottage, was based on a complete fallacy. He might have been stoned out of his mind or he might not, it was not the easy judgement that it looked. He'd been a drinking man for so long it seemed to have no effect. I often wondered why he bothered with the stuff. He always did repeat himself over and over, his speech was always slurred and grizzly, and as for his unsteady walk, that had nothing to do with it at all. After years of working on wet slaughter-house floors, the poor old bugger was bad on his feet and picked his way gingerly from one foot to the other, like a horse on loose scree. In all the years I knew Percy Tricklebank I never saw him drunk or sober, or rather, could never manage to decide one way or the other. He was a rum old devil all his life, and not really my sort of man any more than he was my dad's, but that doesn't alter things by one iota. The very reason I've chosen to start this second phase of the story with Percy Tricklebank is that it could not have begun any other way

Without Percy Tricklebank and his family there might not have been a story to tell – and that's a fact.

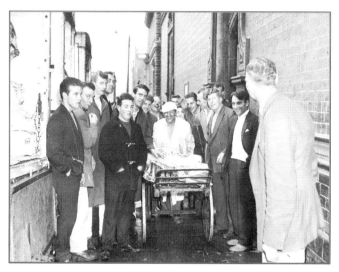

Shutkever the strike-breaker. 1960s. The chap in the duffel coat is Mickey Hawks – our offal lad. Note my unflattering and makeshift (but compulsory) headgear and also the generally friendly attitude despite the seriousness of the situation.

Chapter Fourteen

Wholesale Butcher

•

My first day as a wholesale butcher was pleasant, leisurely, exciting even, but looking back now, I know it for an exact repeat of my first army breakfast, daft as it may seem. After a terrible crossing from Stranraer to Larne, an impossible night on a cold, lumpy palliasse and a wash and shave in icy Irish water, we sat down to cornflakes or porridge, bacon and egg, bread butter and jam, and coffee or tea, and all this at a basic training camp in Omagh, Co. Tyrone. 'Right then you miserable looking lot,' yelled the corporal, 'you've had your false impression breakfast, so now we can start being real soldiers,' thus ruining the whole exercise in one sentence, as only corporals can. That first Saturday ten-years later was, as I say, an exact repeat because all I did for most of the day was watch the slaughtermen, and believe me, they were worth watching.

The scrubbed footballers had vanished completely, left hanging in the changing room with the street clothes, pleasant smiles and mild manners. Dressed only in boiler suits and wellingtons these were Percy Tricklebank's good butchers with steam-lanked hair stuck to sweating foreheads and splashed with blood from ankles to earlobes. I was no stranger to muck and sweat, or work for that matter. Jim Cook and my old dad had seen to that years ago. But Big Bill's gang fascinated me for months to come, so it stands to reason that that first day was a positive spell-binder. If there was anything gory about it, all I can say is that Jim Cook must have inoculated me very well as a boy because I didn't notice it.

I was used to farm work where the pace was deceptively steady, long-distance marathon stuff maintained from morning till evening for two weeks at a stretch until the barns were full and the fields were empty. These men worked in a fury, pieceworkers paid by result, a different technique entirely, which I found both breath-taking to watch and downright dangerous to be involved in. Yet there was nothing haphazard about it. One man would place a cleaver in position a few seconds before another would reach for it almost without looking, all with little or no verbal communication, mainly because it was unnecessary, but also because it was practically impossible. Cleanliness called for hot water by the bucketful, and the water tank was steam-heated by a pressure pipe that sounded like a very angry motorbike. Then there were two electric hoists that screamed and clattered, and an electric splitting saw that went down the length of a bullock in about five minutes and kicked up an unholy fuss the whole time. Add to that the crashing of the iron gate as the animals came thundering in, and the staccato crack of the killer's gun that followed shortly after, all enclosed in an area no more than eight-yards square and there's the picture – a Hell's kitchen. And in that steamy-hazed, slippery-floored confine were seven busy men, keen-edged knives and choppers galore, and anything up to four tons of wet, greasy, deadweight beef; a seething, dangerous bedlam that would give most farmhands claustrophobia for life. One hour of watching Big Bill's gang churning out meat in Birmingham abattoir, and a long-cherished myth that only country-men knew how to work was banished forever.

The only real job of work I had that day was a grand little number for a man of my qualifications. In the lairage, on the floor above, were the five loads of cattle I had delivered the previous day, and when the killing pen was empty I had to go up the long, concrete slope and bring down another four. From time to time I went to inspect the market stall, no longer the empty shell of the previous day and fast filling up with rows of steaming sides of beef, the muscles and nerves still twitching and jumping in a most ghoulish manner. Old Harry and Percy Tricklebank were buzzing about wiping the odd smears and stains off and generally tidying up the rows. The sides of beef were carefully graded in sizes and lined up to the fraction of an inch – in those days there was tradesmanship and pride in everything.

As the beef came in, the rollers passed over a section of rail, connected to an overhead scale and the check-weighman was entering the weights in the 'hot-weights book', sticking tickets on the sides stating the code number and the weight. There stood my dad, splendid in a spotless white coat, generally sussing things out ready for Monday and puffing at a very large cigar, American style – hygiene madness had not yet arrived. Hides were being stacked and counted, heads and offal loaded on to special trucks to be wheeled down to the fridge, and fats and by-products all graded and collected – what they call a hive of activity. And Shutkever & Son were only a very small part of it. All ten slaughterhouses were going full blast, churning out lamb as well as beef, and that's not counting the piggery at the other end of the market which, to be truthful, I hadn't yet seen myself.

Birmingham Meat Market was to be a very busy place for the next twenty years. Nevertheless, that first Saturday, from my point of view at least, was an absolute oasis of calm when compared with the following

Monday when, at a time when most sane and honest citizens are still tucked up in their beds, I thought I'd dropped into a madhouse – and for weeks after, I still wasn't sure that I hadn't. It started at a quarter-to-six with nowhere to park the car, and this despite the fact that the market was not officially open for another fifteen minutes – and from then on it got steadily worse.

Not being strong on adjectives, I'm not sure that I can do full justice to the situation but it was surely the biggest business mess in modern history. Around that time British Leyland were taking some stick one way and another, but rest assured, compared to Harry Shutkever's initiation into wholesale butchering, they were the very acme of business efficiency. I mean it – the bare fact that we survived is a source of bafflement to this day. By the time I found my way back to the stall, my dad was surrounded by men I'd never seen before in my life, trooping along rows of beef and sticking wooden skewers in the meat with no time to talk to me at all. Eventually there came what could be termed a lull, no more than thirty seconds I swear, but it was enough for my dad to swoop in close and point across to our second stall.

'Go and sell the lambs,' he said. 'Take two shillings a pound for 'em.'

I suppose I was lucky in a way because there was no pork or veal to confuse the issue, only sides of beef and lambs on that first day, so even I had no difficulty telling which was which. I know this all sounds daft, as though I'm trying to be flippant or attempting to squeeze some humour out of the situation, but that's exactly how it was. Before the previous Saturday, I'd never seen a dead lamb or a side of beef, and now they'd had time to dry out and stiffen, they'd changed in appearance even since then. So if I can admit to not knowing a lamb from a calf, how was I ever to distinguish between a good lamb and a bad lamb, an old lamb and a young lamb, or even a big lamb from a small lamb? The answer is that I couldn't, not then nor for some time after, because it takes years to become a judge of meat and even then there's room for argument. Just the same, that was it. My dad pointed across and I became a lamb salesman, all in a minute.

There were one-hundred and twenty lambs hanging in rows, neat as soldiers, and the fact that I sold most of them in the next hour would suggest I was a very good lamb salesman, but only to the uninitiated. The truth was that my dad's two shillings a pound was too low, and if I'd had any brains at all, I'd have realised it by the speed at which the lambs were going and charged a bit more, perhaps a lot more – feeling the market, it's called. What had happened was that all the good lambs had been snapped up and the fifteen or so left were the dregs, although as I have said, I couldn't see the difference. It never occurred to me to drop the price by a penny or two. My dad had said two shillings a pound and that was that. What I should have done was charge two and fourpence for the first score or so and slowly eased down, until by now I could have taken one shilling a pound for the rubbish and still have averaged out at my dad's two shillings. But of course it's easy to be clever twenty years after the event, when I was a real meat salesman.

I now realise that most of the butchers were in roughly the same predicament as myself; those with businesses dating back less than fifteen years most certainly were. For that length of time, rather than going to market to buy their meat, they had simply waited at the shop to accept whatever the Ministry of Food allocated to them, and their housewives did much the same. All in all then, it was very much a case of the blind misleading the blind, the main difference being that they did know what they were looking at, whereas I didn't.

As well as selling the lambs, I was weighing and booking them, one main ticket and three carbon copies, and the process of lifting the lambs from their hooks and hanging them on the scale deposited enough grease on my hands, and the tickets, to render my biro inoperative. Not a good start. Having selected and bought his lambs my butcher was anxious to see them loaded on to his van and race off back to his shop, and usually the longer the delay, the shorter the temper. It must be fully understood that fourteen long years of meat rationing had just ended. The British public had gone meat-crazy and it was no time for a butcher to be kept hanging about at Birmingham Market a moment longer than necessary. This brings us to the real problem. There was only one meat porter (or humper, as we called them) between the two of us, and my dad had a queue of his own, all waving ten-bob notes about in a determined effort to stop him from straying over to the lamb stall. I soon became desperate enough to begin carrying lambs out to the street myself, and in so doing discovered a major problem. At eight o'clock the slaughtermen started work on the next day's cattle, which meant that not only did they need me to drive the cattle down from the lairage, but also there was an urgent need to create some space on the stall. Once started, the new sides of beef kept coming in a mass-production type flood. It might have slipped my mind but Old Percy's butchers were not only good but extremely swift, and being on piecework, were apt to scream the place down if held up for more than thirty seconds. Just to make things more interesting, the check-weighman failed to show up and must have decided after last

Saturday that the job wasn't to his liking, because we never saw him again, not even for the day's pay we still owe him.

Luckily, just as I was trying to scheme out how to be in three places at once and still manage to sell the last few lambs, help arrived in the form of Robert the office clerk; another ancient in his seventies, although he didn't look it. This being the first week, he had no money to collect and no ledger work to do, but happily, unlike the check-weighman, he turned up just the same. He'd been in the meat trade all his life (and at Birmingham Market, if I remember correctly), knew all the butchers, who paid and who owed, was quite a respectable meat salesman and positively lightening with figures. I'll go as far as to say that what Percy Tricklebank did for the slaughtering side, Master Robert did for the sales. It all boils down to the fact that we were badly understaffed, which was borne out by the fact that, twelve months later, with the mad days over, so that we'd settled down rather than expanded, we had three humpers, two offal staff, two scalesmen, a drover and a check-weighman – all extra to the numbers in that first ridiculous week, and busy men every one.

The fault must be laid fairly and squarely at my dad's feet. Cattle hadn't changed, not even in price. Weights and measures and money were the same (that, they're not now) so that from a purely trading viewpoint he was, as they say, very much on the ball. But I'm afraid in all other respects, my dear old dad had got badly out of date. First of all, in his day there were no such things as 'humpers'. The slaughtermen started work at six, carried meat out till the market closed at ten, and then went into the slaughterhouse for the rest of the day. It was the same with office staff, more so even, because deep down inside, my dad looked on anybody who wasn't actually producing, as dead wood. In his book, one good man on the stall should be able to do all the weighing and booking, after which, when the market closed, go up to the office and do the ledger work, wages, and anything else, which was how it always had been before the war.

My dad's grandest miscalculation, however, had to do with trade unionism, and although I will set down his views as they affected our business, and also confirm the fact that, like him I am a wicked Tory by persuasion, I am not anti-trade union, either in principle or in practice. Truth to tell, until 1954, Trade Unions were something I vaguely remembered reading about in history lessons, mainly to do with cotton mills, coal mines, hunger marches and all that. I'd forgotten about them. I thought they didn't belong in the real world. My dad was a little better informed, although I'm afraid it didn't help very much. He was of the opinion that all it needed was a few serious strikes to see the unions out of funds and broke, so that right-minded men, bosses as well as workers, could get on with the business of earning a living and leave all that nonsense where it belonged – back in Russia where he came from. Actually in his particular case such thoughts were reasonably based, because he never suffered from labour relations trouble on account of his being what was called a good gaffer: a carrot man rather than a stick man (except with me!) He was clever about it mind, no hypocrite either, and never gave the impression either by word or deed that it was a charitable institution he was running. I can best demonstrate this by explaining his hide bonus scheme, a typical example of my dad's coaxing method in full swing.

The slaughtermen, as I have said, were paid on a piecework basis, and being men who liked to earn plenty (if only to waste it in the pub) there was always a call for speed. The removal of hides is a tricky business and the knives used are keen to a most terrible degree, so it was always on the cards that these valuable items could become badly holed in the process of removal. Needless to say, leather with cuts in it is of little use to cobblers or anybody else, so cut hides were down-graded severely. My dad's system was to pay a shilling for every first-class hide on top of the normal rate, paid in the form of a bonus at Christmas, very useful at that expensive time of year. As first-class hides were worth some four-shillings apiece more than seconds, the scheme cost us nothing and was also an incentive in more than the obvious way. The back-end of the year was the time to make money, so it was also a time when slaughtermen were in strong demand and it was not unknown for rival firms to indulge in a little underhanded bribery to coax men their way at such times. With something like seventy or eighty pounds each in the kitty, in the form of my dad's hides' bonus, there was little danger of our men being tempted, not till after Christmas anyway.

That was just one of many devices in my dad's repertoire designed to keep his men happy at their work and, even if they were mere devices, they were all clever and they all worked. Hard and fiery as he was, and he was never a one to mince matters if anything or anybody displeased him, if all bosses had been like my dad there would have been no need or desire for Trade Unions in the first place. The sad outcome was, that over the years there were several industrial skirmishes, and whenever a stoppage of work occurred we were up to our necks in it, along with everybody else. My dad grew to despise Trade Unions and the more they pushed him about, the harder he hit back so that, although the hides' bonus and one or two other things stayed, bit by bit, the rest of the perks were withdrawn and Louis Shutkever became no different from any other boss: no worse but no better either – I think it was sad, anyway.

It was trade union trouble I got myself into on that first day, through carrying lambs because, unbeknown to me (as were most things), and although I'd never heard the expression, much less recognised him as such, on the very next stall to us was a shop steward. He came in close, and as he thought, menacing. 'If I see you carrying meat out again I'll call all the men out.' I didn't even know just what the threat implied but felt I had to say something. 'What's the trouble?' – although he didn't appreciate it, my enquiry was actually genuine. 'The trouble,' he said, 'is that carrying meat is a job for a humper not a bloody clerk.' I might have been a bit green (understatement of the year) but after a year or two with Harry Wooton and his like, there was little danger of my being cowed by a scruffy-looking bugger like Joe next door. I looked him straight in the eye and said, 'I think you've got it wrong somewhere mate,' as conversationally as I could manage. 'I only look like a clerk – actually I'm the managing director.' All true, not a word of a lie, but I must admit it sounded a bit on the grand side – even I was impressed. Just the same, I decided to be more careful in future, so although I still carried meat out to keep the odd customer happy, I always made a point of handing any tip I might have received over to our professionals (who always accepted).

To get back to where I was, once the slaughtering had started I became the drover again, and between Old Robert and myself the check-weighman's job got done as well. In this vein, meat salesman till ten and general dogsbody for the rest of the day, I was so busy at the market that the next couple of weeks just vanished. I didn't even manage to attend a single cattle market. Unlike all the other staff shortages, the lack of a market drover was not one of my dad's oversights because he had, in fact, found a drover and taken him on: the trouble was he was employed by another firm and needed to work his notice. Our market drover elect was known by the unlikely title of Captain Skimmer and I'll explain how he came by it in due course.

Captain Skimmer was about sixty-years of age, tall and heavily built, boss-eyed and ugly as sin, and must have stood at the very top of the tree as far as market characters were concerned. He could just about read and write, but make no mistake; he was nobody's mug, which I discovered right from the start. Although he knew who I was, because my dad had introduced us, and although he knew he was coming to work for us on the following Monday, and although he could see the desperate state I was in, trying to do half a dozen jobs as well as being the market drover, he never lifted a finger to help. In fact, on at least two occasions, the exact reverse was true. With me running my legs off attempting to head off cattle about to take a wrong turning, he stood there looking the other way as though we didn't exist – even when one of my bullocks nearly trod on his foot.

'That's a rum old bugger you've taken on as a drover,' was how I summed up the situation to my dad shortly after. 'He must be blind as a bat and deaf as a lamp post.'

My dad was unimpressed. 'You don't understand Captain Skimmer, that's your trouble lad – there isn't another like him anywhere.'

Amen I thought. He was a crafty old sod all right, was the Captain and worked on the simple principal that if I got myself into enough trouble without him, I'd appreciate him more when he arrived. In his own way, he was very cute and needed to be, I can tell you. In those days everything went mad; we couldn't buy enough, kill enough, sell enough, and more important, as far as the Captain was concerned, our allocation of lairage space couldn't hold enough. The lorries came in from the sales and (once he'd started, that is) whatever came racing off – cattle, sheep, calves, or pigs, were his responsibility until needed. All had to be kept separate, killed as required, and entered correctly in the 'hot-weights book', and all depended on Captain Skimmer's system being fool-proof.

To this end, he had little nooks and dens all over the place, ingenious some of them, like the muck-chute for instance. Provided it wasn't too full he would lodge three or four calves there safe and warm overnight, but had to shift them a bit smart next morning, before the corporation men started work. Captain Skimmer's attitude used to vary from absolute despair: 'What can you do Gaffer? ...one pair of hands? ...what can you do with only one pair of hands?' to rank superiority, 'you're lucky you are – you've got Captain Skimmer. Some of these kids as call 'emselves drovers could skin you in a week – lose the town they live in some of 'em could.'

What's more he was right. It's amazing how many animals (lambs mostly) went missing overnight at Birmingham Market and were never seen again. Some hadn't even arrived. The drovers simply hadn't counted them properly. There was no such danger with the Captain – he could count all right, and remember what he'd counted. He was a real case was Captain Skimmer, and we were lucky, just as he said (over and over). As for his honorary title, that was interesting, not only because of the way he got it but because it was my dad who invented it many years before.

It was quite common for the cattle buyers to go to Banbury by train in pre-war times, mainly because there was no alternative, but also because they played cards (Solo was the game) and on a good day could earn the day's expenses before they arrived. It so happened, that due to a derailment somewhere in the night, their train was held up halfway to Banbury. It also happened to be at Easter, when the spring lambs were coming on the market and in great demand, and as the lambs were sold first, there was always the possibility they'd arrive in time to miss them. Something needed to be done and done quickly. My dear old dad solved it by sending a telegram to the chief auctioneer –

'Hold sale,' it said. 'Captain Skimmer held up on train – coming for lambs.'

At Banbury there were hurried consultations, resulting in a delaying tactic that was British to the core. The lamb sale couldn't commence because the auctioneer couldn't be found, and small wonder – he'd locked himself in the lavatory. (There's ingenuity for you). In the meantime, the head man himself, that old Scotsman I told you about, not only ordered a taxi, but went in it to meet the delayed lamb buyer. Eventually the train pulled in.

'Which one is he, Mrrrrr Shhuuutkever?'

'Which one is who?' My dad, I'll have you know, was a bundle of fun in those days.

'The lamb buyer? Captain Skimmer?'

Hubert Royston (his real name) knew nothing about it, of course, but nevertheless stood there grinning, one eye to the east and the other to the west, not three yards from the taxi door.

'There he is,' said my dad pointing. 'That's Captain Skimmer. Come on. I'll introduce you.'

Needless to say, Hubert Royston remained Captain Skimmer till the day he died.

Stratford Market – Christmas Show late 1960s

(I'm second from the left with one of our staff, Harry Lowe, in dark jacket next to me. Despite the fact that most of the people shown are long gone, this same picture appeared in the Stratford Herald for many years. Either they liked it so much or more likely they couldn't be bothered to go and take another.)

Chapter Fifteen

Big Guns

•

If the captain of the QE2 had suddenly been handed the command of a creaking old canvas-driven four-master, in a full Bay-of-Biscay type storm, many people would be left wondering just what he would do. But I wouldn't be amongst them. Because, as it happens, I know. Our gallant seaman would have to learn a whole group of new skills in record time, or be remembered mainly for the heroic way he drowned when his ship went down. I know what I'm talking about, believe me, because a similar choice fell to me in July 1954, and my storm blew on at least until the end of the year.

After six years of dedicated practice I could now talk to farmers as easily and effortlessly as my dad. In some respects I was even better at it because I knew more about practical farming than he did. The knacker-cow trick was still the same, as was the store cattle business, and both carried on in the background as before. That, however, was where it ended, because everything else I'd learned about the cattle business had suddenly become out of date.

Modernisation usually means simplification. School children no longer need to scribble in the margin because they have calculators – but simplification need not necessarily be good for everything and everybody. From July 1954, weigh-scales were introduced into cattle markets and the cattle were sold at so much per hundredweight rather than so much each. The effect of this was to place the bad or mediocre judges on a par with the good judges, and after six years of applied concentration, I was beginning to place myself, rightly or wrongly, among the latter. All for nothing now it seemed. Yet where I would have welcomed a bit of modern science there was nothing, because when it came to assessing the meat value of animals, there were neither ministry graders nor anything else. Rather than being simplified, or modernised for that matter, the whole thing had shot back a generation and now called for a skill level that would most definitely separate the men from the boys.

It's small wonder my dad could hold his own with ministry graders, Lichfield George's, and all the rest of them because, up till then, I'd had no idea of his actual capabilities. One quick look at a bullock was enough to tell him how many pounds of dead-weight meat was standing there in the field, and its selling and eating quality, all within a pound or two and no guessing whatever; the same with sheep or calves. He wasn't so good with pigs because he'd been trained as a kosher butcher, but he wasn't over-long picking that up either. It was sickening, frustrating, and not a little frightening to realise just how far behind I was. Light-years it seemed, and every day something or other would occur to rub it in deeper and deeper. So perturbing was this inferiority complex which, as you might or might not have gathered by now, was somewhat alien to my nature, I decided to do something about it, and chose a most dramatic method indeed.

Sunday was cattle sorting day, when the cattle from both farms were rounded up, sorted, penned, loaded, and transported to Birmingham, ready for Monday's kill. I would pick out a bullock and challenge my dad to a duel of judgement to see who could get closest to the animal's carcass weight; half-a-crown a time. All serious stuff. I wrote my assessment on my bit of paper, after which he told me his. Then came a delay till Monday to see who'd won. It might have done some good if I could have afforded the full course, but it soon became apparent that I couldn't – financial suicide is not too strong a word for it. To add insult to injury, my dad not only continued to relieve me of my half-crowns, he insisted I dash off to the canteen to buy him a cigar with it, so there was a shoe-leather loss as well. I did win once, but as it happened, there was a registered complaint and a steward's enquiry, followed swiftly by disqualification because, between Captain Skimmer and the checkweighman, two bullocks had got mixed and the wrong ticket was stuck on the wrong bullock. My dad didn't like that at all, giving me one of his terrible stares that said: 'Are you trying to kid me lad?' After which, he begrudgingly gave me the benefit of the doubt, pointed out the right bullock and claimed his cigar with his usual good advice:'You shouldn't gamble lad'. The Captain and the checkweighman didn't get away Scot free either, and were collectively treated to one of his 'good cussins' for their trouble.

Veal calves were another branch of the trade I was particularly weak in, never having bought a calf before in my life. So I tried to learn the calf business by the same desperate method with, I'm sorry to say, the same tragic result. My dad was far too hot for me. I kept parting with my halfcrowns and, what's more, it was doing him no good either, because he was smoking too much. The scheme itself however was basically sound, a stretch of the brain does nobody any harm. All that was needed was an easier victim, someone my own size so to speak, so when Big Bill Tricklebank volunteered for the post, I decided to take him on.

If anything it was still biased against me, because Big Bill had been killing and dressing calves for years and, unlike me, did know something about them. In the initial stages, I found myself handing out halfcrowns at a rate of about three to one, but it's my belief that eyesight and observation are no different from arms and legs: the more they're exercised the stronger they become and I'd been living off my eyesight for years. Bit by bit I began to get the hang of it, and the halfcrowns began to trickle back. It even became something of an embarrassment so that I wished we'd never started it, and reached the stage of deliberately over-estimating now and again, just to level things up a bit. Suddenly came a change. Big Bill started to come up trumps time after time. It was costing me about a quid a week and I was beginning to wish we hadn't started it for a different reason altogether. He was taking the calves out through the back of the slaughterhouse, weighing them on somebody else's scale, then hanging them on our stall and calling me in for the duel. Needless to say, that was the end of that, but I've written this in only because it leads on to the next adventure, and in no way to discredit Bill Tricklebank. The truth was, he did it out of pure devilment, and furthermore, everybody on the firm, including my dad, were in on it. Part of my training, that's what it was, and I was to be very thankful for it in the near future – almost immediately in fact.

The auctioneer at my Monday grading centre (defunct now of course) had always been friendly in his attitude, and by way of repayment I'd promised to attend his sales in the new era, which I was then doing. What's more, in order to build the sales up, I made it quite clear that I was prepared to bid on anybody and everything to get things going and was doing that as well; cattle, sheep, calves, the lot. But when I started attending a Tuesday market, the calf buyer from a Birmingham firm, who I'd set about, along with everybody else on the Monday, came up to me before the sale.

'I hope we're not going through the same nonsense as yesterday?' he asked, quite legitimately as far as I was concerned.

'I explained all that, didn't I? I promised Sam I'd give him a leg up for the first few weeks and I'm doing it. It's different here. I come here to earn a living and if you behave yourself you'll get no trouble from me.'

He only bought calves incidentally, nothing else, and that market was one of his main sources, because it was in a predominantly dairy-farming district and there were always plenty of calves on offer. To us, the calf trade was something of a nuisance. There was never much profit in veal and although we had to have some to please our customers, it probably amounted to about thirty or forty a week, no more than that. When the calves started selling he was soon in the thick of it and I left him alone as I said I would. He didn't bid on me either but there was no need, because every time I tried to buy a calf, a rat-faced chap in a peaked cap set about me in some form. It was something like the Harry Wooton affair at Gloucester, except that the whole thing was Lilliputian in scale; these being calves rather than full grown cattle. I didn't even know the man, where he came from or anything about him, except that I didn't like the looks of him, which was easy enough to be sure. The farcical thing about it was that I didn't really want any calves and if he hadn't turned nasty, I would probably have bought a couple at the most, and then only for the fun of it, just to keep my hand in. But old Rat-Face seemed to be begging for trouble, and when he started chucking his weight about there was nothing for it but to accommodate him. Truth to tell, if I'd known a bit more about the calf job I'd have thoroughly enjoyed myself. As it was, I did my best and was instantly made grateful for that crash course on calf judgement, despite the halfcrowns it had cost. The outcome was that I finished up with four calves at a rather terrible price and he had quite a large dose that couldn't have been any better. But that was only the beginning.

My Tuesday Market was neither large nor small, and rather than having a proper canteen there was a mobile affair, parked in the front yard quite close, as it happened, to where the calves were being loaded. After the sale I stood there, having a ritual tea, and watched the transport men sweating for a living, and because the tea was hot, I had time to notice a very interesting phenomena, very interesting indeed. All buyers have their own marks, sometimes cuts in the hair with scissors or else dabs of marking paint, and I noticed that Rat-Face's calves were not only mixed up with the ones carrying my Birmingham friend's mark, but were being loaded onto the same lorry. In a few words, what had happened was that I'd been taken for a ride, two-timed, as they say. My Birmingham pal had talked me into leaving him alone, then set his dog on me in the person of old Rat-Face; not nice at all. I was a bit put out by it, sufficiently so to go looking for my pal to tell him, and was lucky enough to catch up with him just about to board his car. I leaned in through his window and although I'm well aware that I look nothing like Robert Mitchum blind drunk, that was the impression I most wanted to create.

'Watch your step next Tuesday, Mister. You won't be pulling another stunt like that on me I can promise you!'

I'm absolutely certain I didn't look remotely like Bob Mitchum, but the outcome was rather remarkable just the same. One way or another, I must have frightened him out of his wits because he didn't come either to that market or to my Monday market ever again. His firm sent someone else in his place. What it boiled down to was that they'd decided to set the big guns on me, in the person of an old, pre-war calf specialist who was to attend my Tuesday market with orders to eat me alive. After my years with Harry Wooton I'm afraid he had no hope whatever, and although a somewhat hectic 'battle-of-the-calves' was to take place in the following months, there was also a comic aspect to the whole thing.

Big Guns was a man of about sixty or so with short-cropped grey hair in the best sergeant-major tradition, a barrel chest, and a speech impediment. He stuttered badly especially when excited or angry. He was also a long-standing drinking buddy of Old Percy Tricklebank, who came with me to the Tuesday market, as much for the ride as anything else. The joke was that Big Guns didn't drive, and the moment Old Percy found out he was going to market by train, he straight away invited him to come in my car instead. It was quite a long ride, perhaps an hour or so depending on the traffic, and all the while those two old mates were chatting away about things they did a century or so ago; some of it, quite good listening I might add. Once at the market, and in among the calves, we went at it like Hell. Big Guns and myself that is – Old Percy was firmly entrenched in the boozer by then. Afterwards, we all got back in my car and off we went back to Birmingham. It was the funniest war ever.. I still have to laugh when I think about it, and what's more, I know for certain that I won it hands down.

First of all, as my dad quite rightly said, calves are the easiest of animals to judge and I soon got the hang of it. In fact, it's not buying calves that's difficult but rather selling them, because veal is inclined to dry up and must be sold quickly. The second advantage lay in the fact that Big Guns only bought calves and nothing else and, what's more, his firm needed them whereas we didn't, so I was batting with the wind all the way. Straight after the calves there were usually a couple of pens of goats which I could more or less help myself to, and even if Big Guns didn't realise how cheap they were, psychologically it did me good.

The main thing that beat Big Guns, however, was the man himself. He was not just old-fashioned; he was positively quaint. His idea of fighting a war was to starve me to death. A war of attrition – imagine that! There he was, absolutely determined to buy every calf in the place, when I was more than happy to take them to the top and drop out, in the old, time-honoured way. I simply couldn't go wrong, and just for good measure, the farmers all thought I was a grand chap and kept stuffing ten-bob notes in my pockets for helping them along. I might have dreamed it all. It was certainly good enough, but as it happens there is still a living witness and every now and again, I go and ask him.

It all came to an end in the classic manner. Old Big Guns came to me in Birmingham Market on the Monday (actually with his hat in his hand), said he'd had enough and asked what was needed to call it off. I told him how easy it would be. All he had to do was give Rat-Face the sack, buy his own calves and leave me in peace to buy mine; which was how it happened the very next day. So although I won the war, I suppose I lost the peace because the ten-bob notes stopped coming and understandably so; the poor old farmers couldn't understand it at all and went home crying their eyes out. Rat-Face tried to put a brave face on and look as though he didn't care, but take it from me, he did. His best racket was in bringing a few calves of his own and slipping them onto his pal, and seeing all that falling by the wayside must have been highly misery-making to a low-life of his calibre.

I've given it a lot of thought since, and remembering all those tax-free ten-bob notes, I can't help wishing old Big Guns was alive today and doing his best to starve me out the way he did, back in 1954.

Farmers' Glory

•

If I look out of my window to the far side of the yard, I can see a yellow machine. In fact, I've no need to look… I know it's there because I was using it this very morning. It's a long way from new, the sides are made of wood and it's about as old-fashioned as I am but nevertheless, although (like me) it creaks a bit, it still works. What I did this morning was to load that unsightly collection of chains and slide-bars until the main body was full (all in five minutes, and sitting on my behind on a hydraulically equipped tractor) then tow it down the fields, select the right gears, and in no time at all, about four tons of cow muck was spread evenly all over the place (and some down my neck).

The name of the game is muck-spreading, and even with the help of that yellow monster, it's no laughing matter; so take it from me, back in the un-enlightened 1950s, it was a very desperate business indeed. The first operation entailed attacking a yard full of straw-bound and heavily trodden cow muck with a hand fork and plonking it, forkful at a time, onto a trailer (and before that, a horse-drawn tip-cart). It was then transported to the field and deposited in long rows of heaps, until the whole field was covered and the bullock yards empty. The final task was to then wade into all those heaps with that same hand fork and fling the stuff about, until the whole lot was evenly spread and the heaps had disappeared. It was by no means the worst job that came round every year because, for one thing, in the depth of winter it was a grand way to keep warm, but it wasn't the best either, and there are dozens of osteopaths still getting fat as a result. By the first muck-spreading, after the return to wholesale butchering, it was February 1955. We had survived our first Christmas and I was beginning to see where most of the problems lay, even if I couldn't find the answers. I had also got to know Bill Tricklebank a lot better and, strangely enough, it was the muck-spreading business that did it.

Big Bill was born at least a hundred years too late and in the wrong place because, I say in all seriousness, he should have been a cowboy in the old West. I'm not implying that he was silly because he wasn't, neither am I saying he was childish, because he was anything but. Nevertheless, I soon came to realise that many of the antics he got up to were based (unconsciously perhaps) on incidents in westerns – the pub fights for certain. What's more, he had all the attributes that would have made him a very good cowboy. He was strong, agile, good with animals, an excellent shot with a rifle, and when it came to throwing things, I never saw anyone better; sticks, stones, ropes, or anything – he could knock a fly's eye out as they say. He even walked like a cowboy, his long, lean, broad-shouldered body slightly hunched in the 'Tricklebank stoop' and those lanky legs covering the ground much faster than they looked. Everyone called him Big Bill (his dad always abbreviated it to 'the Big 'Un') and that's what he was. Yet to my mind, that big frame was so sparsely covered that he could have been two-stone heavier and looked all the better for it. He was about ten years my senior.

As soon as the day's kill was done, Big Bill would come onto the stall, face clean and shining and hair stuck down flat (he'd just had a dip in the water tank), then stand tall with hands on hips (a sheriff making an arrest), and defy anyone to even suggest that the carcasses could have been dressed cleaner, better, or quicker than he and his gang had just done. In this, incidentally, he was absolutely safe. On Saturdays, for instance, they worked straight through and were capable of killing more cattle before breakfast than some gangs could manage in a day, and not a single tear or nick to be found anywhere. My dad, Old Percy Tricklebank and Big Bill were proud of the butchering that came out of our slaughterhouse, and I can say without fear of contradiction justifiably so. 'No Rubbing Rags' was how Old Percy put it that day outside his cottage, and believe me he was dead right.

I happened to mention that I had a busy week-end lying in wait at the farm, and although still in a sweat from his labours, Big Bill surprised me by offering to come out and give me a hand. Mind you, at the time he probably didn't know what he was letting himself in for because, as I've since come to realise, prejudice can work equally well in either direction. Until I witnessed the frenzy of that first Saturday morning in the slaughterhouse I'd never dreamed that city men could really work, and to a man like Bill Tricklebank, the notion that a boss's son could actually sweat his week-ends away in farm fields was totally alien. Whatever he was expecting to find I'm sure bore little resemblance to what was waiting for him on that fateful Saturday afternoon. There they sat, row after row of brown, similarly shaped piles of cow muck, all neatly laid out in straight lines from one side of the field to the other. (Make no mistake, I was a man of no small pride where my muck heaps were concerned.) Apart from them, the only things in the field were him and me, both armed with a four-tined muck fork, and a few inquisitive birds – magpies mainly. He took the one row and I took the next and away we went, a simple matter of jabbing our forks into the piles and coming away with a loaded fork, which was then flung and scattered into the spaces between the heaps. And yet the outcome was to surprise the pair of us.

I've already said that Bill Tricklebank was big and strong, and with a streak of viciousness in his nature that added to both, so make no mistake, he could have torn me to pieces with his bare hands. Yet he couldn't keep up. I didn't slow down and I didn't race either, just plugged away as I always did, but when I reached the far end of the field and looked back, poor old Bill was possibly at the halfway mark. I worked my way back to meet him and we had a good laugh about it, then went back to the beginning of the next two rows and started off level again.

This time he took more care about it and before we started, had a searching look at each row to decide which one to call his. Just what it was he was looking for I wouldn't know. All the material came from the same place and was plonked there by the same hand, so if the law of averages means anything at all, there was absolutely nothing to choose. He flew at it like a jet taking off, grunted and groaned and put everything he had into the effort, will-power as well, but it did him no good at all because I left him standing again. I'm not bragging now, anymore than I was showing off then. It really was a surprise, a shock even. I couldn't have stood up on that greasy slaughterhouse floor, never mind work there all day in rubber Wellingtons. On the few occasions I'd been called on to sort through piles of cow hides, it was all I could do to drag them from one pile to another, so how I'd have got on, holding them up with one hand while carefully taking them off the carcass with the other, is anybody's guess. Yet when it came to a simple thing like slinging a bit of cow muck about, I had Bill Tricklebank hopelessly outclassed and, what's more, he admitted it to my dad that same day.

My dad was not amused and although he laughed and made little of it at the time, the first chance he got, he told me just how unamused he was. 'Ought to know better lad – I don't want Bill tired out and buggered up with your farming nonsense. I need him fit and happy on Monday morning.'

He could look for trouble anywhere, could my old dad. In any case Big Bill was happy enough on the following Monday morning although, to be sure, he lost no time warning the rest of the gang: 'Don't go into the muck field with him whatever you do – he'll kill the bloody lot of you...'

The author making and laying a hedge

Big Tom

•

To any who think this part of my story is being monopolised by the Tricklebanks, I'm afraid I have some bad news because any moment now, a further two are about to make their entrance – the oldest and the youngest.

Making money the hard way, which is what we were doing, has several drawbacks. One of which being that it's so demanding physically, there's no time to realise how well you're progressing. The one sure way comes as a form of shock. Just when it seems there's a few bob in the kitty, the Inland Revenue start reaching out for it, and that's when you begin to know. The first reaction on my dad's part was to have a most unholy row with our poor old accountant, a man so mild and soft spoken I couldn't help but feel sorry for him. To be fair, my dad was provoked because not only did their plate-pushing demand drop on us out of nowhere like a meteorite, if we'd been daft enough to pay it, we'd have been broke to the wide. Our old accountant was no fool and nearly managed to convince me, so that I nearly managed to convince my dad that we weren't spending enough, or as he put it, '…our legitimate expenses were ridiculously low'.

When I say he nearly convinced me I mean that, although I could see what was necessary within the system, I couldn't agree that the system was correct and what's more, I still can't. If a firm can buy, kill, dress and sell, and all they require every week for say £400, for the life of me I can't see why it should be necessary to spend £500 per week to save money doing the same thing. Which, in essence, was what our accountant was advocating.

Nothing is all bad, and one outcome of this financial mess was that my dad was eventually convinced that our old lorry, the third by the way (although similar in most respects to the other two), had got to go, and be replaced by something better. And how much better! Not second hand, not home-spun, not petrol driven, but a real live, brand new diesel motor with a massive, professionally built cattle body (complete with roof), sheep decks, partitions, spring assisted ramp – the works. Our name was emblazoned across both doors and the front panelling above the cab, in beautiful signwriter's lettering that cost so much I was frightened to tell my dad and had it smuggled in with the rest. Sad to say, by this time, things had changed to the extent that I no longer had time to drive cattle lorries about and, apart from the Sunday work, private deals and knacker cows (which could be done in the evenings), all our market transport was being contracted out to the professionals. This was where the youngest Tricklebank made his entrance.

Young Jim Tricklebank was completely different to all the others, except, that is, if he lost his temper; when the difference was not so complete. He was quiet, serious minded and never would have anything to do with the meat business. He didn't even eat meat – a vegetarian would you believe! Old Percy must have done his nut when he first found out. He had a high-school education, which was more than I had, then went to work at a dairy farm in our village and consequently wasted it. Luckily for us, his boss was a bit on the tight side where wages were concerned and Jim came to work for Shutkever and Son already a trained farmhand (which was very useful), and absolutely bursting to become a cattle-truck driver. He was hard working, conscientious, sober and honest. He worked for us for years and to this day, if I'm stuck at haymaking or any other time I ring him and he comes (and brings his son as well).

I have dealt at some length with the slaughtering set-up because from a practical point of view it was the key to everything – not the real key mind – Louis Shutkever was always that. As it happened, the killing side worked fairly smoothly for years and if we weren't the envy of the market on that score, I know for sure my dad always thought we were. It was a different story on the stall, however, and there the big bogey was the humpers; always argumentative when present, and always absent when needed. This humper problem became even more irksome when, shortly after the market opened, one of the firms closed down and their stall space was re-allocated. So now we had three stalls, and although we always hoped for more, we never got them.

The ridiculous start with just the one humper was doomed from the off. Before the first week was out, we'd found two more, and what a dance they led us! To be fair, the original one was a good enough chap. He'd worked in Birmingham Market for many years, knew his way about and was polite to the customers. But he was too old and too small for the job, certainly for the mad pace of those early months and he soon left to open a butcher's shop of his own. The other two were real shockers; lazy, argumentative, and extremely bolshie to boot. They were also a bit on the light-fingered side, although this must be seen in perspective because it's an accepted part of life in a wholesale market that if you can't look after your stock you positively deserve to lose it.

The two main trouble spots were (and probably still are) basic to the humping side of the meat trade, and if ever there was an anthem written for meat porters, both of these aspects would need to be included. The first is their uncanny ability to vanish just before a rush of customers arrives, and once gone, they take some finding. Humpers are absolutely ingenious at finding new cafés and hidey-holes when you think you know them all.

The market opened at six and closed at ten, leaving us just four hours a day to get our meat sold, so if there was time to spare unearthing skulking porters, trade had been bad. The other problem was to do with the business of tipping and, in my opinion, far more serious than the first. I disapprove on principle, and think that a man, or woman, should be paid for doing their job by their employer, and only receive extra gratuity for activity not included in their normal work. Which is no doubt how it was envisaged in the first place. Even so, I must clarify that it was not the extra money I begrudged our humpers but rather the effect it always had on their performance.

Unfortunately, some of our best and most important customers, butchers who spent four or five hundred pounds a week and paid promptly every Monday, thought the same as myself, and if they did tip, it was just the token half-crown or so. One butcher actually used to hand out small pork pies as though they were the crown jewels, which only added insult to injury, because not many paces away a firm sold pork pies and the men could pinch as many as they could swallow. Equally irksome were the other sort, butchers who only dealt with us after failing everywhere else, bought a lamb or two after an hour's haggle and were often a month behind with their cheques. These were the sort of jokers who ruined the whole thing by waving pound notes about like there was no tomorrow. Believe me, nothing was more sickening than to see our men tumbling over themselves to dance attention on these yobbos when real, solid, bread-and-butter customers were kept waiting on the stall, getting angrier by the minute and threatening to take their business elsewhere. They didn't just threaten. Sometimes they did it.

My dad didn't frown on this practice. He positively did his nut over it. To his way of thinking, customers were an endangered species, every one sacred beyond words. He loved them all, the real ones that is, the other sort he made use of in the same way they used him. We ran what's called a 'high-class trade', not a brag, merely a description, and a good cross section of our customers lived in middle to upper-class houses, some way out of town with the odd paddock or small field for the children's ponies –

the gin and tonic belt I think it's referred to nowadays. While they might have been good butchers, in the main from a rural point of view, they were rank amateurs and these small plots were often well out of control. They all knew we owned a farm because it was printed on our bill-heads and it was not uncommon for such men to ask my dad's advice in these agricultural enigmas. He didn't know the answers anymore than they did, but it made no difference, because he did much better of course – he sent me over to sort them out. I've ploughed, worked, planted, rolled and harrowed dozens of acres of grass for the benefit of butchers' kids' ponies, and repaired fences, and done odd jobs, and all for sheer love. I'd never have dared accept a single penny from any of them, in case my dad found out. He'd have skinned me alive. There's a more practical way of demonstrating this salesman-client relationship – the wretched business of sucking-pigs.

At Christmas we dressed the stall up and put on a bit of a show – not just us, the whole market was done up like a Christmas tree. Actually it was the men themselves who wanted it more than the meat firms, and although quite a few butchers came for a walk round on the Christmas Sunday, the larger percentage was always made up of the men and their wives and families. Dressed up in Sunday suits, most of them were unrecognizable, even the butchers, who normally did their buying disguised in old macs and cloth caps. And every year, one or another of the firms either side of us would have sucking pigs as the centrepiece of their displays, propped up in a sitting position, with oranges or small apples in their mouths and all the jazz. This would set the butchers thinking and before the morning was out, one or two of 'ours' would ask my dad to find them a sucking pig for their own Christmas show. And, of course, they were never turned down.

Now I don't know what the general public's attitude was (or is) to sucking pigs, and don't know what they taste like, because the rabbi wouldn't approve, but I can say without fear of contradiction that the majority of farmers hate the idea in its entirety – 'baby murder' they call it, and I'm inclined to agree. Nevertheless, my dad had said they'd get them and that was that. It was no easy task I can tell you, but if an intensive enough search was made and enough money offered, sucking pigs could be found. The case in mind was on the first Christmas after the great opening, when my dad sent me thirty miles to pick up two little pigs that were so dear they couldn't have earned us a button, no matter what he'd charged for them. If there was another business anywhere at all where the customer was so highly prized I've yet to see it, and even now, thirty-years later, if I'm kept hanging about or otherwise feel neglected by shopkeepers or the like, I get annoyed enough to clear off and take my business elsewhere. It's not that I am standing on my dignity. I just can't abide it. Anyway, these last few sentences should be enough to establish just how much the attitude of our humpers went against the grain with my old dad, but fortunately we didn't have to tolerate it for very long because, when Percy Tricklebank's oldest son came on the scene, he hit us like a cyclone and put a stop to all the nonsense once and for all.

Everything I have said about Bill Tricklebank was true. He stood over six-feet tall, was broad as a barn door, lithe and agile and strong as a lion. So when I say his big brother was some three-inches taller, and could give him full sixty-pounds in weight, it should be appreciated that I am talking about a very large man indeed. Big Tom, which is what everybody called him, was a man-and-a-half, in every sense of the word. I'd never met his like and don't expect to again.

I am not small, about five-feet-ten-and-a-half, and although I stand reasonably straight, and he had that characteristic stoop of all the Tricklebanks, I came up to his chest and had to crane my neck to look him in the eye. My poor old dad didn't reach much above his belly button but, rest assured, he used to tick him off just like all the rest of us. It was the funniest spectacle ever. Big Tom always adopted a sort of raised eyebrow, quizzical look while my dad tore into him ten-to-the-dozen. We all had to laugh, even my dad was often forced to join in. Tom's body was more lumpy than beautiful, certainly not of the Charles Atlas mode, and in street clothes, he looked deceptively normal for a man of six-feet four, but in a boiler suit and at work he was massive. He had a boxer's face, broken nose, not ugly but somewhat pugilistic-looking, long gangling arms, great big hands, and like his dad, flat feet that gave him some trouble. When Old Percy told him he'd found a good man to doctor his feet, Big Tom's unsmiling query was: 'What's good about him? Does he do 'em while you wait?'

He never would work in a slaughterhouse, although his dad told me he'd tried everything (including his belt) to get him to change his mind. Before coming to us he drove a meat transport lorry, and continued to do so on a part-time basis. Incidentally, he was a very good swimmer and as a boy of fourteen was awarded a medal for bravery after swimming across a canal to rescue some horses trapped in a warehouse fire. It was virtually impossible to remain angry with Big Tom for long, on account of his individual style. He could cut my dad off in mid-stream simply by tickling him under the chin and saying '…now then my little chickadee, you'll do yourself a mischief if you carry on like that.' As I say, my poor old dad had to laugh, although he tried to look the other way while doing it. The other item, which cannot be left out, was physical strength. There are men who look strong and men who are strong. Birmingham market was not short of either, but Big Tom Tricklebank was in a class by himself and rather than rave on about it, I'll relate a couple of incidents that are true to the letter.

As a transport driver he delivered meat from Birmingham Market to shops in the surrounding districts and arrived one day at the doorway of a well-known Birmingham butcher, who was also a life-long friend of my dad. On Tom's back was a large bull hindquarter, and for the record, they go up to about two-hundred and fifty pounds apiece.

'Where do you want it, Gaff?'

'Up there'll do for now,' said the boss, pointing to a hook high up in the wall of his somewhat old-fashioned shop. Most butchers, it should be said, have a fairly well developed sense of humour and this one, no different. He was pulling Tom's leg but before that day was out, he had good reason to wish he hadn't bothered. Tom didn't say anything. He walked across to the shop wall, gave a grunt and a heave and half threw the hindquarter on to the hook where it stayed, lodged firm. I've actually seen that hook, in fact I don't think I ever managed to visit that shop without having it pointed out and the story re-told. Believe me, it's heavens high. At any spare moment during the rest of that day, the butcher and his staff tried to get the hind down but couldn't budge it, and finished up climbing the wall with a ladder and hacking it down, a piece at a time.

The other tale was much closer to home because we were the victims ourselves. On the advice of our insurance broker we purchased a safe for the office, mainly for petty cash and wages, because the bulk of our business was by cheque and not really dangerous from a burglary point of view. It so happened there was an auction sale-room on the other side of the street, almost across the road from the office, to be precise, and my dad bought a safe there for the princely sum of ten pounds. All that remained was to get the thing into our office; a job for the humpers who paraded over complete with meat trolley with which to do the deed. To load it on the trolley and wheel it across the street was no problem, but our office was not on the ground floor. First, there were two flights of stairs, steep as a thatcher's ladder, gloomy as a catacomb, and no handrail whatever. Big Tom carried that safe up on his back and plonked it down in the middle of the office, all in a minute, and it took three of us best part of half an hour to wriggle it into a corner. No doubt in some nearby pub, Tom was laughing into his pint of mild, knowing full well that he could have dropped it there in the first place.

Tom Tricklebank was a great man and much loved by everybody, especially those he came into contact with on another of his spare time occupations. He was a coach driver, taking people on day trips and things, and the antics he got up to were nobody's business. I've seen photographs of some of Big Tom's travels, one of which is a real classic. It showed an ancient and isolated little pub out in the wilds of North Wales, with sheep grazing in the background and the normal stone wall along the front, and perched along the wall, like swallows on a telephone wire, were a line of elderly people of both sexes – and it doesn't take much imagination to work out how they got up there. The coach driver was in the foreground, but not posing for the camera like the rest. No fear, he was topping up their glasses from a forty gallon wooden barrel on his shoulder. I know for a fact that rather than miss the fun, when Big Tom was at the wheel there were many who simply refused to go with anyone else. But what I liked best about him was his total unflappability, and the fact that it was virtually impossible to offend him, or at least so it always seemed. I refer now to the almost continuous dialogue between Big Tom and my dad, much of which could (in many men) have been taken at face value and led to trouble. Mind you, I know also that Tom thought the world of my dad in spite of everything.

Thieving, as I have said, was an occupational hazard in Birmingham Meat Market, and no doubt, in every other meat market; mainly I suppose, because it's so easily done and the spoils so easily disposed of. Had there been less butchers willing to accept stolen meat there would have been far fewer thieves among the men. To aggravate matters and increase temptation there were no doors or windows, no partitions whatever and internally the place was wide open. Only two options remained. Anything thought small enough to be smuggled out had to be sent down to the refrigerators below (which weren't ours and charged at so much per pound per night), or hidden away by hanging it among the overhead rails – 'skying it' was the term. On a Thursday morning we finished up with an odd back of lamb that my dad told Tom to sky in the aforementioned manner. Next morning it had gone.

'Now then Tom', said my dad, who incidentally, seemed to notice anything missing before he'd got out of his car. 'What's become of that back of lamb?'

It was more than just an inquiry. With my dad's way of glaring, it was almost a direct accusal. Tom's reactions could easily have been quite different. But Big Tom was Big Tom. The only one of his kind I'm quite sure. He stood there like a rock, close enough to be towering over my dad, and looked him straight to the eye with the calmness of a nun.

'They don't call me "fingers" for nothing Gaffer,' was all the change my dad got from Big Tom Tricklebank. No temper, no fuss, and left to make of it just what he liked.

I know it's another cliché and I don't care a button – Big Tom Tricklebank was what's called a gentle giant of a man, and we all loved him.

A Farming Discussion

•

Although I said I'd never been inside Birmingham Market prior to 1954 it wasn't strictly true. I had been there once or twice as a child. The practical result, however, is the same and it would probably have been better for all concerned had my dad not taken me. I didn't like the smell for one thing, and as with most children, death was scary; believe me all that dead meat frightened me out of my mind. Those were the two reactions I remember, dislike and fear, and they might have been obvious enough to establish in my dad's mind that the meat trade was not for me. There was however one other thing I remember, and that was the mystery of the coal miners. They walked about the sales hall and abattoir in brown overalls, peaked helmets with lamps set in the front, powered by battery packs fastened to their heavy leather belts. It never occurred to me to ask my dad about them, mainly because he was a bit on the heavy side – a children should be seen but not heard-type of father. In any case, what I was most interested in was hampering him as little as possible, so we could be out of there and back in the car that much the sooner. It perplexed me just the same. What were coal-miners doing strolling about in a meat market, and with their lamps switched on even though it was broad daylight and above ground to boot? But of course, they weren't coal-miners at all. They were meat inspectors, and I mention this now, because for the epic about to unfold, it's important to know what manner of men these meat inspectors were (and still are).

First of all it must be understood that we needed the meat inspector, and for many years were extremely fortunate to receive the benefit of their time and knowledge completely free of charge, although to be sure, we didn't realise this at the time. Some ten years or so ago Birmingham City Council found itself hard up and borrowing with both hands, and the fact that it had nothing to do with us didn't help matters a bit. They decided to saddle us all with an inspectors' fee – half a crown per beast, one shilling per pig, and nine pence per lamb (if I remember correctly) and that was when we first realised just how lucky we'd been before. We didn't take it lying down of course. Any time a group of us got together within earshot of a city councillor, we gave voice collectively and in loud and ringing tone. 'The inspection of meat is a service to the public,' we said, 'and, as such, should be paid for out of the rates,' we said; but however right we were (or weren't), it made no difference whatever. Inspectors' charges don't cost votes, and in any case, once the Markets and Fairs Committee had tasted our money, it was all over.

The meat inspectors were a serious-minded, well respected bunch on the whole, and best likened to football referees – nobody loved the poor devils, but we all knew the game could not be played without them. The very thought of selling diseased meat for children to eat is enough to send a shiver down my back even now, and I'm quite sure that would apply to any meat wholesaler I ever met. (It was always the children we worried about, never their moms and dads.)

Just the same, a shake of an inspector's head could, and sometimes did, cost real money – seventy or eighty pounds for a bullock – and although there was insurance available, it was so prohibitively expensive and complicated that we (at least) stood such losses ourselves. No compensation of any sort was paid and even our tame knackermen couldn't help, because all meat condemned in Birmingham Market was compulsorily burned and that was that. So now we know the type of men we're talking about, and a little of the part they played in the scheme of things, we can return to the story.

I have already made the point that to do business with farmers calls for a degree of patience. It's no use trying to rush the job because, providing they like you, farmers like to talk – and if they don't, you're wasting your time anyway. I'm not claiming this as a hardship because in most cases they are intelligent and humorous people, so that as well as being necessary, these conversations could be mutually enjoyable and quite often educational. Besides, what's better than a cup of tea and a good old rattle when factory workers are boring themselves to death screwing up nuts and bolts till five o'clock? One of my farmers was a great talker, and the subject that often came into our conversations was the local Farmer's Discussion Group, of which he was a past chairman. So exciting did he make the thing sound that I must give him half the credit for my eventually becoming a member, only half mind; the other half I claim for myself, because I had a scheme you see. Why not mix business with pleasure? Others seemed to manage it? Why not go along and enjoy these wonderful meetings Fred keeps warbling about, and who knows – might get to know a few new farmers and buy their cattle from them? The outcome was that I delighted old Fred by ringing him to say I wanted to join, and the following Tuesday, we went together in my car for the enrolment. Strangely enough, although I was a member and regular attender for the next fifteen years (and even became chairman for one year) I never saw him there once.

The Farmers Discussion Group was very much like a Young Farmers' Club but with one important difference. The young farmers insist on a top age limit (twenty-five I think) whereas our lot made no such imperious demands – to be able to afford the yearly subscription (five shillings or thereabouts) and walk in through the door was all that was required. If we changed our meeting place from one pub to another five or six times during my years of membership, it was for none of the usual reasons. Farmers and sons-of-the-soil we might have been, but we were also as highly civilised and well-behaved a bunch of 'persons' as one could hope to meet. I did almost everything I set out to do. I went on informative and useful farm walks in the summer, enjoyed some very interesting meetings during the winter, and made a host of new friends among the local farmers. But there, I'm afraid, it ended. I never bought a single cow, pig, sheep, or calf as a result of joining that group. It seemed the better they got to know me the more they shied away – so much for charm. Just the same, I was glad I joined because I learned a lot from those meetings, and it wasn't all farming. I learned to stand up in front of a room full of people and bellyache at the top of my voice if an element in the nights' discussion went against the grain, and also how to heckle if the speaker gave enough cause – two arts that have come in mighty handy ever since. I also learned that if you stay in a group long enough, you become a committee member, a little longer still and you become chairman. Both noble positions that fell to me, the experience in each case being well worth any minor inconvenience caused. I also learned something of my fellow man as well.

I was not the only oddity in the group. There was a corn merchant, a retail butcher or two, and if I remember correctly, a transport manager, but most, if not all of the rest, were genuine working farmers of one form or another. Now although every man has his own methods – or his dad's that he's inherited, and although there's a big difference between say, dairy farming and pig farming, the gulf is not wide enough to create much in the way of mystery between one branch of the industry and another. All I'm trying to say is that they probably knew each other's daily routines down to the last forkful, whereas with the likes of myself this was not the case. From the many hints, remarks, and innuendoes it slowly began to dawn that, where my trade was concerned, there were topics and areas where some of those good people had got hold of the wrong end of the stick. One in particular kept creeping in, more in leg-pull than with malice I admit, but irking just the same, so when we sat in committee, working out a programme for the coming season, I saw a chance of killing the thing off once and for all and jumped in with both feet. Not only did I suggest a tour of Birmingham Meat Market one evening, but offered to do the honours as guide. Everyone thought what a good idea it was.

The two main worries that closed in, as the appointed evening drew near, were first, that nobody would turn up, and second, that I might find nothing to say to those who did. In the event, I need not have worried. About three dozen members actually assembled at the main gate at the arranged 7.30pm, an average turn out for an outside visit although in one respect much better. A normal assembly would have been made up of at least thirty percent wives and girl friends whereas for my evening there were no ladies whatever, so had the mixture been of the usual order, I might conceivably have broken all attendance records.

As for the other anxiety, it was clear almost from the start that even if I had managed to prepare a written programme (I did try but gave it up as a bad job), I'd never have had the chance to use it. The moment we walked inside the main gate the thing took off and went almost by itself. I marched them all up the concrete slope into the lairage, showed them how well we housed our animals for the night – clean straw, hay, water, the works – then led them step by step through the whole sequence, until we finished up standing among the sides of beef in the sales hall. Such was the interest and curiosity in the smallest of details, we had to miss out the piggery side and the cold store completely and I could quite easily have arranged a second visit without covering anything twice. There was, of course, the deep down pleasure that my evening had been a success, on top of which, one of my secret motivations had already been accomplished. It has always been my impression that farmers think we only need to buy their animals and press the magic button and hey presto – solid gold. So now, if I'd done it anywhere near right there were at least three dozen who knew otherwise. Another was their often voiced misconception that once killed and dressed, there was so little to choose between bullock meat and cow meat that we could, and did, sell it all as best beef – hopefully I'd managed to knock that on the head as well. All that however was merely a by-product. The one that had triggered the whole thing off all those months ago was still in the box.

As well as being an abattoir and meat sales hall, Birmingham Market had an important subsidiary role as a school for meat inspectors. My dad even had his suspicions about that. If, because of a run of bad luck or perhaps through natural causes, we had more than our usual share of condemnations he would say, 'Look out lad, we're in for it again – must be exam time and they're looking for specimens.' Who but my old dad would have thought of that? I had mentioned my proposed walk to the chief inspector some weeks before. First to ensure he had no objections and second, in the hope that he might have something to offer in the way of padding in case I ran out of ideas. The good man not only gave me his blessing, but actually volunteered to stay behind and show us round the school; a gift from the gods if ever there was one. So that's where we went for the last half hour, into the meat inspectors' den, the lecture room; a place as unique as it was unexpected, and not even known about by many who actually worked in the market. This was because although the entrance was just inside the main gate, it was hidden behind the porter's lodge, almost as though they were ashamed of it. Yet with its array of beautifully preserved and presented skeletons of small animals and birds, all housed in individual mahogany framed glass cases, its masses of written data and pickled specimens, it was a most fascinating place and I know my farmers were taken by surprise by watching their faces as they took it all in. The inspector did his job like the true professional he was, showing them everything from bovine tuberculosis to what looked like black tennis balls, but were in fact hair-balls taken from calves' stomachs. By the time he'd answered their questions, freely and fully, the big problem was going to be bringing the thing to an end. I'm sure he could have gone on all night and what's more they would have let him. I strongly suspect there were more than a few surprised vets in our district for the next month or two.

However, with our half-hour in the inspectors' lecture room stretched to over twice its intended length, I finally succeeded in calling a halt. Then, in the time-honoured way, someone stood and proposed a vote of thanks for an interesting evening, which I accepted in what has become something of a set piece over the years. I then thanked the inspector for his time and trouble and the evening was almost over – but not quite.

I had done exactly what I set out to do but still wasn't satisfied. I'd played my ace in so gentle a fashion, there was a very good chance of it going unnoticed and that wouldn't do at all.

'There's one thing more. Before we go, I want you to take a good look at Mr Frazier here and think hard on what you see. Then cast your minds back to any discussion we've had about the meat business over the years, but remember to keep your eyes on the inspector, because it's important that you do. Right then – how many times has it been hinted to me that all we meat chaps have to do to keep out of trouble with meat inspectors, is to drop them a pound or two? Well now – there he is, have another look and tell me – how many of you would fancy your chance at bribing Mr Frazier here to pass diseased meat on to the public?'

It might have been in bad taste, although I don't think so. Everyone enjoyed the joke and laughed quite heartily, the inspector included, and it was fairly obvious that the evening had ended as well as it had gone right from the beginning. But I'll say one thing – they never did it again.

The Customers

•

So what about the most important part? I've written about myself and my dad, cattle and cattle markets, the meat trade and some of the staff, but there's something missing? Surely the most important part of any business are the customers, the shop butchers; why haven't I given any space to them? Well the answer is that it's more difficult than it seems. Most of our customers were smart, well-educated, honest men who knew what they wanted, bought it as cheaply as they possible could, and paid their bills promptly every week. They ranged from the city centre man with a large passing trade, through the family butcher with the corner shop and the regular order customers, to the man out of town, the village butcher who was supposed to kill his own but didn't. They were the back-bone of our trade, solid citizens all, and apart from thanking them for their custom over the years there's little else I can say.

So that leaves only the others; the sharp-shooters, the tearaways, the duckers and divers, right down to the outright thieves, and if I say too much about them it will sound as though they were in the majority, which was certainly not the case. So I'll take the middle road and put down a few of the interesting cases and the antics that made them interesting, and be so careful in hiding the identity of the persons concerned, I'll most likely finish up offending everybody. We'll start with a simple case.

At Easter time spring lambs are dear, not only for the housewife but for the wholesaler as well, but such is the demand that we all (wholesalers and retailers) searched the district for some that at least wouldn't lose any money. Little can be done at the auction sales except to keep calm, because people are falling over themselves to buy. It's just as awkward trying to buy on the farms. The farmers themselves don't know what to ask and do what they always do in those circumstances – ask plenty.

So obviously the key to success, or at least survival, must be at the other end – the selling end, and the big secret is in the weight; not an ounce must be allowed to escape. Spring lambs must be killed as soon as possible because without a constant milk supply they 'melt like butter in the sun' (an old but true quote). The real trick, however, lies in the dressing, and this is where a bit of tradesmanship on the part of the slaughtermen can keep the boat floating. Not only should nothing be unnecessarily removed from the carcass, but as much as possible must be skewered back on in the form of 'fancy dressing'. Kell fat, mudgin and one or two other odds and ends, all fixed in place, so that, believe it or not, it looks quite pretty, and don't forget, every ounce counts. In his turn, if the retailer wants spring lamb in his shop early in the season and at almost affordable prices, his best bet is to buy 'fronts'. These are the lower priced halves and comprise necks, breasts and a few chops, rather than 'backs' (legs, sirloins, best end chops), but spring lamb just the same.

My tale concerns a well-known Birmingham butcher who did just that, bought a dozen or so fronts of spring lamb, gave the humper a couple of bob to see them safely on his van, then went about his business elsewhere. The humper went to the exit gate but the van he was supposed to meet hadn't arrived, so rather than push the trolley all the way back, explained the situation to the nearest salesman, told him who the fronts were for, obtained permission to leave them where they were, and went in search of the van-driver. Meanwhile, the butcher himself had completed his round of the market, arrived at that same stall and spotted the trolley load of fronts. Immediately his eyes lit up, (fronts of lamb were his speciality all the year round, never mind Easter), and after looking them over as casually as he could, asked the salesman his price. You wouldn't get very far working a meat stall without a certain amount of devilment I can assure you, and this one was no different from us all. Without so much as a blink he named his price and struck a deal. Now spring lamb must be handled very carefully, else there's a real danger that all those bits and pieces so carefully and artistically skewered on by the slaughterman will shake lose and, God forbid, drop off altogether. This had not only begun to happen, but was the reason that the butcher, a clever man by the way, hadn't recognised the fronts in the first place. Butchers also have a trick or two when necessary.

'I only want the fronts Bill,' he said, after the deal was done. 'I'm not standing for all this rubbish – you've got the kitchen sink stuck on here.'

'You know me – anything to oblige. Take it off if that's how you feel. I'm not going to argue about a bit of fat, not with a good customer like you.'

And that's just what he did, pulled of every bit of the trimmings that, only a short time before, and a few yards further up the market, he'd had weighed and booked to his account. Needless to say, he wasn't hysterically amused to then be told that he needn't have them weighed because they were already his. I'm not trying to make the butcher out to be an idiot because he was anything but, in fact it's really his story and if he hadn't told it to me himself, I wouldn't have known of it.

A more serious affair was much closer to home because I was involved in it up to the neck. It concerns the wretched business of dissatisfied customers and what to do about them. Nothing is ever absolutely safe and sure in the meat business. However carefully bought and handled, animals can get bruised or 'shaken' sometimes so deep in the meat that nothing shows until the butcher starts jointing up. Sometimes it's the weather that upsets the applecart, a thundery or sultry night can start the meat 'turning', unless it be artificially chilled which ours was not. One way or another then, there was always a risk of trouble which must be faced up to, talked out, or put right, if a customer was to be upset, offended or, Heaven help us, lost altogether.

My dad was surprisingly easy-going at such times considering what a hard-head he was with everything else. Often as not, he would merely ask the butcher how much he thought he was out of pocket and instruct the clerk to credit the amount there and then. I've seen him do it for quite large sums and not turn a hair. A customer was always worth more than a few pounds bruising allowance to my dad. That's how he saw it, a nuisance and nothing else. In any case most butchers were more apologetic than annoyed, and would usually bring the trimmed out bruising back the following week just to show their good faith. My dad would pat them on the back and tell them to forget all about it. Needless to say, I had little choice but to do likewise. He'd have skinned me alive if a customer was lost through such a matter and, in any case, I agreed with him, so between us we handed out allowances and tried to keep laughing the whole time.

I had built up a friendship with a butcher while I was the lamb salesman, kept him when I moved to the pork department, and introduced him to my dad in the meantime. He had two shops, both high-class and busy and was spending something in the region of four hundred pounds a week with us, a good customer and a nice chap, and in fact one of the few butchers I'd mixed with sociably. He rang from his shop one Tuesday morning, asked to speak to me, and said he was very sorry but a hindquarter he'd bought from us the previous week was 'bone-tainted' (a not-rare-enough hot weather problem that made meat smell to high Heaven). My normal reaction would have been to ask him, over the phone, how much he thought he'd lost and credit him with it, and for the life of me I still don't know why I didn't. Instead, I said I would be passing his shop on my way to the cattle market and I'd call in. I really don't know why I did that. I've often tried to puzzle it out, his shop wasn't even on my way to the Tuesday market, it was miles out and only vaguely in the same direction. However, having said it I had to do it. He met me at the door full of apologies. His shop man had made a mistake, it wasn't our meat at all and he'd rung the market to stop me coming but I'd already left, and so on. I tried to laugh it off and in an effort to show how unruffled I was, asked to see the bad meat just in case my expert opinion might help with the real culprit. And that was where I made my big mistake, although to be sure it would have ended in tatters sooner or later (he says with hindsight). He pointed across to some bits and pieces stacked on a tray but wasn't at all happy with my offer and from the doorway I could see why.

To be absolutely blunt about it, what had happened was that my pal had seen us handing out credits from time to time without making a fuss and decided he could do with a few pounds-worth. There was no other possibility. He had no bad meat anywhere in the shop, not from us nor anybody else, and when I said I'd come over he must have panicked. On the tray he pointed to, there was meat from more than one animal. It was two different colours for a start and even from a distance I could see three shin bones. He'd tried to scrape something together to show me but couldn't. He sent his cheque through the post the following Monday and was too embarrassed to come anywhere near us again. We lost a good customer on the most false of pretences ever.

It's probably true to say that the smaller the value of the things he sells, the smaller-minded becomes the salesman himself. A man who sells paper bags at tuppence each can't go giving pennies away in the process, so perhaps I'm to blame more than anyone for a small niggle I level at butchers in general. After years of doing business with farmers and cattlemen, and at a quantity scale wherein twenty pounds here or there was never an obstacle, butchers on the whole appeared to me to be small-minded. (Not all of them, for God's sake). They'd walk around that old market for so long to save a half-penny a pound that the time and shoe-leather would often be worth more, and for infinitesimal amounts I've seen them leave perfect sides of beef, in preference for others not in the same league. I know I'm being unfair, and to them it's my thinking that's at fault, so perhaps it's just as well I've never had to earn my living behind a butcher's counter. Nevertheless, there's an example of petty-mindedness on behalf of a Birmingham butcher that I can't leave out, and the fact that he was one of the bigger fish, a chain-store man, makes it all the more ridiculous.

My dad was an excellent draughts player, and just for the record, there's more to that silly little game than meets the eye. He taught me, and although I really should have left a blank space so as not to write about the pair of us in this context on the same page, I'm no idiot at it either. It was quite a popular game with several of the market men, and providing there was no rush to go to auction, it was not unknown for either or both of us to be found whiling away the odd fifteen minutes playing draughts in the canteen. Some of the butchers could also look after themselves on the draughts-board, but some couldn't, and the one I'm thinking of really belonged in the second of these categories but wouldn't own up to it. Let's not forget, we are talking about a man with several top-class shops, many in fact, a handsome, well set-up man who would not look out of place cruising the Adriatic on Niarcos's yacht. He was also in the same age group as my dad and they'd known each other from way back.

They used to play draughts occasionally, and although it never showed on his face, my dad was in dead trouble every time. The problem was not the one normally expected, the exact opposite in fact. My dad was always hard-put ensuring the other chap won at least half of the games without him realising it. It's not so simple as it might seem. I know this because from time to time I was daft enough to find myself in the same position. Furthermore, in my case it was positively desperate because whereas my dad could win or lose as he saw fit, most of the time I was under strict instructions: 'Watch what you're doing lad, if old Donald Duck is in the canteen and you get playing draughts for Christ's sake see that you lose. I've got six sides of beef I'm trying to sell him. If you can't do anything else kick the bloody table over'.

I did say it was ridiculous, didn't I? We never played for money, only for practice; and there was this wealthy, successful, and indeed clever, man who could be made so happy by winning a game of draughts that, all things being equal, two or three hundred pounds-worth of meat sales might depend on the outcome. What's more, one of his pals was a good player and knew exactly what was going on but egged him on just the same, making the whole silly exercise a hundred times worse. Now there was a nasty edge on an already miserable situation. If he got himself into so bad a mess that even I couldn't save him, he'd start talking to his pal to make out he wasn't concentrating, and yet if I did manage to lose, he looked at me as though I was Mohammed Ali, unconscious on the canvas with all his teeth knocked out. It reached a stage when I stopped going into the canteen completely unless I was sure he was elsewhere.

I don't really like writing about fiddles and rackets because although I'm safely out of it by now, I still have friends who aren't, and just in case there are men in the market who don't know all the tricks, I would hate to be the one who taught them. However there's one that's a real darling. It's been going on for years and, to tell the truth, I wouldn't know how to stop it. What's more, it's not practised by butchers or business men at all. This is one for the lads.

Every Friday they (humpers, slaughtermen etc) come on the market looking for meat to take home, and sometimes perhaps to sell to their mates. They pay cash, come in handy for clearing up the bits and pieces, and in any case it would be a very mean man who refused to sell meat to market staff. This trick is diabolically cunning and works just as well with fronts of lamb, legs of pork, or anything of the sort. They buy a small one, in the case of a front of lamb it could weigh fifteen pounds or thereabouts, they pay for it, get a receipt, everything open and above board, but they don't take it home. The reason it's bought on the Friday is because they've just been paid and have the cash, but it's not really needed until the weekend so it's put in the fridge overnight. Oh yes! It's easy enough to guess what comes next. On the Saturday, they take one twice as big. Simple enough to be daft, but in one form or another, it's gone on for years. I should say at this point that I'm talking about the old market (my market) and the situation could now be different, but I've a sneaking feeling that old soldier is still lurking about in the concrete jungle of the new place.

Then there's the story that's so well known it must give the game away, but then again perhaps it needn't. The inside story is far better than the one generally known and well worth including. It concerns a man so skint it was unbelievable, and everything he did to conceal it made it appear worse. He wore a bowler hat for one thing, and striped trousers, carried a rolled up umbrella and a rolled-up newspaper, so that from either side he could be mistaken for a gent from that other market. I never saw his shop but I know he had one, yet although it couldn't have been over-big because his needs were tiny, in the early days, few wholesalers would risk serving him. Once again my dad's weakness for eccentrics might have saved his bacon (as it were) because on our stall he was never refused. Now everybody has heard of men who struggle for a living. My dad himself had done it for years, but in this particular case I'm half inclined to miss some of it out because it's almost unbelievable (like the man, his bowler, and all the rest). His day went something like this.

In the morning he came to the market to buy his meat, then scampered back to open the shop and try to sell what he'd managed to buy, nothing unusual about that – all butchers do it. In his case the difference came after closing time because he wasn't only a butcher. In the evenings he played piano in a pub or club or something, and I don't mean mess about at it – by all accounts, he could play. From chucking-out time until the market opened next morning he should have had some time to himself, but not him – at night he was a night-watchman at a factory. For most of the time I knew him that was his normal routine, and he kept it up for years and seemed quite happy doing it, and I nearly forgot something else. He fancied himself at the dogs and by way of appreciation for being a willing supplier, he used to whisper racing certainties from behind his paper into my dad's ear. I should also say that despite everything I've just written, he paid his bills on the dot every week and as far as I know we never had to chase him for a shilling.

The end of the story is where I must be careful because this is the bit that was publicised in the local papers. He came into a great deal of money very suddenly, a whole lot more than my dad made all his life, and in many ways it ruined him. He put on a lot of weight, exchanged his old bowler for a racy trilby and to me, never looked as happy again, but I could be wrong.

Shop butchers are a volatile lot, at least that's how I found them. For little, and sometimes no known reason, they would explode into fits of temper and disappear forever. Sometimes it's just a bluff. Another firm has managed to coax them to change their allegiance and they don't know how to tell you. I nearly lost a very good, if small, customer for one of the silliest reasons imaginable. A small story worthy of inclusion, if only to demonstrate just how precarious was the lot of the Birmingham wholesale butcher. He was a small, quiet, somewhat unhealthy-looking man, pale as a ghost, nothing like your rosy-cheeked prototype, and no trouble at all to serve because he knew exactly what he wanted and it hardly varied by a spoonful. He was fussy mind, his side of beef had to weigh 260lb. and not much more or less, had to be always from the same side of the bullock, and had to be quartered in his special way. The lambs had to be about 30lb. each, and anything else he bought himself. He came to the market on the same day every week, looked at his meat, said 'Thank you very much,' left a shilling or so for the humpers and that was the last we saw of him till the following week. No trouble at all. Then came the day we made a mistake and after he had been and gone, quartered his side in the normal way instead of his special way, the difference incidentally being one less rib left on the hind. A quandary. Which would be the most acceptable? The right side quartered wrong, or the opposite side of the same bullock (which luckily was still on the stall) quartered right. I took the second option and, believe me, there were murders. That quiet little inoffensive man nearly melted our telephone, the main and most repeated item being that he'd never darken our doorstep again. This incidentally, was long after my dad had gone and I had to deal with it all by myself. I did manage to pacify him somehow or other, although I can't remember how, but eventually he told me what all the fuss was about and it wasn't so silly as it seemed. He had only ever worked in the same shop all his life and the layout was such that without major re-organisation, it was difficult to joint the one side of a bullock and in fact, in over thirty year, he'd never tried.

Then there were the real villains, ranging from the real heavies to the petty-pilferers, all thieves of one sort or another and hardly worth writing about. Fortunately we were not bothered too much by them, and when I come to think just why that was, I'm always led to the same conclusion. After many years in a keen and highly competitive business, I've decided that big is definitely not beautiful, and when it comes to discouraging villainy I'd go as far as to say it's positively ugly. My dad knew every bit of meat on show and exactly where it should be. It's my considered opinion that where there's an actual person running his own business, someone who must be looked in the eye if caught – it seems to put the villains off.

There is however more than one side to this miserable topic, a branch of burglary that ran off at a tangent, so to speak, and that brand of mischief hit us hard. I am referring to dishonest scalesmen, and strangely enough I don't mean our own. There were, amongst the many Birmingham butchers, a certain percentage that I found impossible to deal with, and believe me I tried. Some just didn't come anywhere near us, and others looked and listened but went away as empty-handed as they'd arrived. There were those, of course, who had built up satisfactory connections with other wholesalers, just as had all our own regulars, but there were also the others, not many perhaps but some, and their reasons were slightly more sinister. For a pound note or two, there were scalesmen about who would quite cheerfully under-weigh meat by the hundredweight, and once acquired, such habits become impossible to break. This subject is beginning to depress me and I want done with it, so I'll state my findings on the matter in one short sentence. As far as the meat business is concerned there is no such thing as 'big firm efficiency', and when it comes to buying, selling, weighing or booking meat, the man small enough to do it himself is many paces ahead of his bigger brothers.

I'll conclude with a couple of observations on shop butchers that are of no value whatsoever. We had customers from all over and around our city, and occasionally from other towns as well, yet when one wanted veal they all wanted it, when one wanted legs of pork, so did everybody else, and these trends bobbed up and down for no reason I can think of. It could have been connected with cookery recipes in well-circulated papers or magazines, maybe even Jimmy Young had a hand in it somewhere, but whatever it was, it didn't make life any easier for the poor wholesaler.

Then there was the business of dress. There seemed to be a buying uniform for butchers that consisted of shabby macs, peaked caps, and even slouchy walks, because that was how most (not all) of them came to market week after week. I can take it even further, because after much profound study, I discovered that in nearly every case the dowdier the man, the posher his shop. I used to play a silly game in this respect by looking out for the shops of butchers I knew whilst on my travels, and the amount of polished chrome and tinted sheet glass on shop fronts was an exact contradiction of the men who came to market with their (metaphoric) behinds hanging out.

I drink to all Birmingham shop butchers great and small. They're a grand body of men and I can't think of a quicker way to drive myself barmy than by going back into wholesaling and trying to keep them happy.

City Meat Market & Abattoir, Birmingham, England.
Opened on 26th, December, 1897.
Project now in planning stage for development of New
Markets Centre, incorporating : Meat Market, Abattoir,
Fruit & Vegetable, Fish & Poultry.

◊   ◊   ◊   ◊

J. L. Harper
Company Director.

G. H. Monk & Company Limited,
Wholesale Meat Traders,
City Meat Market,
Birmingham, England.

*Postcard (top – front showing the Birmingham Meat Markett,
bottom – back of card) from G H Monks – 1960s*

Trade Secrets

•

I know my dad always acted for the best and what's more, I must always have known, otherwise I'd never have stood for some of his antics. He had a way of silent accusal (perhaps unspoken is more appropriate than silent) that could be highly vexatious, especially to Yours Truly, who came in for some of other people's share, as well as more than enough of his own. After many years of it I suppose I was more or less immune, although I could never handle it with the same poker-faced nonchalance as Big Tom. Also, I hasten to say, there was a basic difference in the nature of the accusation because my dad trusted me implicitly, and made no bones about it. My signature on a cheque was worth every bit as much as his, with no safeguards or limits of any sort and had been from the start. What's more, there are aspects of market life that are sophisticated to a high degree and also temptations and degrees of honesty, complicated to say the least. There are things that look honest and are not, and vice-versa. An old campaigner like my dad knew them all, taught me about them and we both of us practised them, all in complete trust and knowledge.

What I'm talking about is bribery and corruption, so to those who think that slush money is a recent invention I've some news – it's been going on for years. The trick is in how one goes about it and what it results in.

Bribery and corruption are really the opposite ends of the same thing, in theory at least. My interest, where the meat business was concerned, was anything but theoretical. We'll take corruption first, only because it's the simplest to explain, the nastiest, the more dangerous, and as it happens, the one we had least to do with. Before I say another word I must remind you that this is straight from the lips of an honest founder-member of what could easily have been the most honestly run meat business ever.

Of all the saying and folklore attributable to the meat business one of the oldest and truest states that 'when it's alive it's worth gold and when it's dead it must be sold'; and this is the most valid reason for the likes of us indulging in corruption. It is in fact a good way of getting out of trouble, although by far the best method is not to get in it in the first place, which was my dad's way and also the reason we did very, very little in the way of corruption.

Even with Louis Shutkever at the wheel, problems were not always unavoidable, mainly due to the three-day delay between one end of our cycle and the other, a minimum of three days I should say. Meat on offer today was killed yesterday, which meant it was bought, or at least sent in the day before – three days as I say. So if we catered for say six small customers and only five turned up, there was nothing serious about it, one way or another the remaining meat would get sold. This is the reason my dad preferred to deal predominantly with the 'one shop man', the family butcher, although needless to say all were welcome. On the other hand, if all that meat had been for one large outfit that failed to appear, the name of the game was trouble with a capital T. This really answers both questions. By design, the bulk of our trade was with customers that were 'owner-runners' and if there's a way or a need to corrupt a man who's spending his own money I've yet to come across either. However, a big, hungry mouth to gobble up a stall-full of problems was very useful from time to time. This, I'm sorry to say, meant dealing with buyers not spending their own money, a large percentage of whom (not all, thank God!) would never come close enough, unless tempted in the only way I know. It's a lousy way of doing business and didn't suit my dad at all, mainly because in a way it was admitting defeat.

He would never have contemplated offering cash corruption to a reluctant buyer, because not only did he hate the idea, but loathed the sort of men who demanded it. However, he did have a couple of subtle weapons in his armoury, and would go to considerable lengths to put things in the way of such men. If they were known to be keen fishermen they were offered a free hand to try their luck at our two pools. Some would be invited to accompany him to the cattle markets, and be introduced to important people, which was a play on their ego. And there was always the dog track. With my dad's serious inside knowledge of runners and times, he made sure they always came away winners.

But with the real hard nuts, he moved in an entirely different direction. Providing that the main shops, or chain of shops, was owned by one of his old acquaintances – and that meant most of them – he would contact them direct with an offer he hoped they could not refuse. At the same time, he was not above dropping a subtle, and not always too subtle, hint at what their villainous representative was up to. This tactic was useless in the case of buyers from corporate outfits, which was where most of that category of buyers usually lurked, so he managed without them. He was a proud man and liked to think that people bought his meat because it was the cheapest and the best, and because he was the most pleasant man in Birmingham from whom to buy it. (Actually, despite everything I have said or implied, when he saw the need to turn the charm on, he was a grand chap.)

But that's enough of that. Bribery was much more fun, or I should have said 'being bribed' and we both indulged in it by the ton at every opportunity. Being bribed is absolutely grand, so let us journey together to a cattle market and I'll demonstrate how (and why) it's done. It can start before the sale or during the sale, and even after the sale is not too late, but that is mainly for the less honest, although not necessarily. (I did say it was sophisticated.)

The first thing after arrival at the market is to take a stroll among the cattle pens, and this for many good and sound reasons. Some men like to sort out the actual animals they intend to buy at this stage and have bits of paper or cigarette packets in their hands on which to write the selected numbers, but I was never one of them and neither was my old dad. He always said the best time to judge an animal was when it was standing in the ring, sudden death as it were, and taught me to do the same. At times of shortage, mid-winter for instance, if one's trade is in any way selective, these reconnaissances are useful. Having discovered just where the best cattle are, one knows when to make the effort.

Now all these cattle have owners, and it's a fair bet they're never far away, so when an established buyer (yes – like me) shows himself to be interested in a pen of cattle, it's not very long before he's joined by their proud owner. (This is the tricky bit, I should hate to offend anyone.) The farmer could be a friend of long standing, a business acquaintance, someone you don't know at all, or someone you don't much care for; it does make a difference, although not much – business is business. Sooner or later the farmer is going to say, 'Help me along a bit, they're all good cattle,' or something of the sort; or if he doesn't, he should do because that's what he's there for. It's not then unknown for the buyer to say, 'I'll do my best, leave it to me,' or something of that order, which is as far as it can go at that stage without entering into the realms of real villainy (of which I want no part).

The real artist is now ready to dip in the brush, and takes his place at the ring-side waiting for the start – always the same place by the way – where the auctioneer, and anyone else, knows just where to find him. Suddenly whispered information appears at your ear, such as: 'These are mine Harry, the next four…,' or, 'Mine are coming in next, from 39 to

44…' and so on. There's a more dignified method wherein pieces of paper containing numbers are quietly handed over, which you slip in your pocket and if not careful, forget all about. There's a better way still, when the farmer's lovely daughter comes skipping across with the paper, which must make it more interesting if nothing else. The thing is this; you are being asked, one way or another, to go out of your way to buy specific animals, and what you do about it is entirely up to you. I can only say what I always did and it goes like this.

If I liked the cattle and they were cheap enough, I would have bought them anyway, but just the same, I looked about for my pal and waved his bit of paper about. If he was a real friend, I would go right to the top and maybe a shilling or so more because real friends are rare and shouldn't be neglected. For the rest, there was a bit of gamesmanship, plenty of noise, waving about of arms, but nothing else. It's the next bit that's the most important because after this stage, they are all treated more or less alike. Each one is found, looked straight in the eye and the hand is held out palm upwards in the time-honoured way, although it doesn't always collect anything. This is being bribed, and it's not only tax-free and very nice, but I see nothing wrong in it and neither did my dad. He loved it and what's more, for a long time, we practically lived off it, because until our accountant managed to convince us we were barmy, we drew a weekly pittance from our thriving business that was nothing short of lunacy. Dishonesty only comes in when the farmer's pound note is allowed to influence the proceedings, to the extent that the cattle are bought more for the bribe than for themselves. I'm happy to say this didn't happen in my case or my dad's, and never would have done if we'd gone on for a thousand years.

And now, having jumped the rails a bit, I'll go back to the beginning of the chapter and finish what I started to say. What my dad was in the habit of accusing me of was neglect, and it wasn't so much in what he said as in what he didn't say, or his oblique questions, or his icy glares. Neglect of the business, neglect of the farmers, neglect of the cattle, and because I never consciously did any of those things it could be very vexing indeed. It led to a major row – and I do mean major – and because we were both as hard-headed and stubborn as each other, it blew up out of all proportions and dragged on for weeks. The outcome, however, was not quite what might have been expected, but before I come to that perhaps I should give a couple of examples of the sort of vexation I'm talking about.

It took a few weeks to get the hang of the lamb-selling caper, but from a stone cold start, I think I did as well as anyone else could have done and managed to build up a useful following. One of the things I soon learned was that Tuesday morning was too late to sort out the day's orders and it needed to be done on Monday evening. So every Monday, long after everyone had gone home, found me sorting and carrying lambs from one side of the stall to the other, until all the orders in my book were set out in lots and groups, all ticketed up with the names of the butchers on each group. It was something like an hour's work every Monday (which was a long day anyway) but well worth the trouble because Tuesday's sales were all the smoother on the strength of it. The problem was that some of my dad's best beef customers didn't usually buy their lambs from me, and the reverse was also true. I had rows of lambs marked up for butchers he'd never dealt with. Around Easter time, with spring lambs coming on the market and in firm demand, one of his pals (a man with two good shops), saw some good lambs on my stall but couldn't have them because I'd got them marked up for someone else. He went and complained to my dad and both came galloping over to sort me out. My dad snatched a ticket off one of the lambs and peered at it.

'Thompson!,' he said, 'THOMPSON! – Who the bloody hell is Thompson? I've never heard of him.' It's what they call pulling rank (and him a field marshal and me barely a lance corporal). The lambs finished up on his pal's van, and I was left to apologise to my customer as best I could and try to put him off until next day – it was weeks before he forgave me and then not completely. The worst part of it was that my dad was probably right. At that time of year lambs earn little or nothing and his beef pal was gold in the bank. But the way he did it was wrong and his muttering and grumbling for the next hour left me in little doubt that I was a positive liability, and only his prompt action had saved the day.

The one that really blew the lid, however, happened some time later. It was nasty, underhanded, completely un-called for, and not like my dad at all. In fact, I never found out what prompted him to do it, but just the same, I never really forgave him for it either. I came to work one Saturday morning and a complete stranger was standing on my stall, not passing through, not wandering about, just standing there, and in a white coat similar to mine. I had to ask him who he was.'

'I'm a lamb salesman,' he said, 'I work here.'

I was dumbfounded. Without so much as a word my dad had taken on a lamb salesman and stuck him on my stall. Perhaps I read too much into it at the time, I don't know. It was a shock to my system if nothing else, but one thing I do know is that I was vexed, most sorely vexed, and when one or two other things happened as the days went by, the balloon went up so high it took several weeks to come down and perhaps never did settle back where it used to be. I didn't bandy words with either of them because I did something different altogether, a nose-thumbing gesture it was really, but with a most remarkable outcome.

We had never taken our pork trade very seriously and treated it much the same as the veal, thirty or forty a week, just to please those who asked for it. Our neighbours had a pork stall directly opposite mine, and I'd been watching the performance across the way for some time. They sold an awful lot of pigs every day, at least seventy or eighty and maybe more, and I was quite sure I'd twigged the secret. They only sold the best of their pigs whole or in sides. All morning long they were cutting up into joints, which seemed to keep going as fast as they were cut. I'd been toying with the notion for a few weeks, but the business with the new lamb salesman finally triggered it off. I might as well admit that in those days I had such a bad temper that I was afraid to lose it (I'm well past all that now, of course) and my state of vexation at the time was such that something had got to be done. I decided to become a pork salesman and cutter, all rolled into one, although to be sure, the only training I'd had was watching the bloke over the way.

There were about a dozen pigs hanging at the side of the lamb stall and I started my new career off with them, splitting them down with a big, clumsy beef cleaver and then hacking them into joints. I made the sort of job of which Sweeney Todd would have been mightily proud. The first one I split was such a sorry sight, Big Tom noticed it and came over to show me how it should be done. But however badly I did it, by nine o'clock they were sold, all twelve of them, and when I skimmed through my sales tickets and did a quick calculation, they came to some fourpence a pound more than if they'd been sold whole in our normal fashion. This was very encouraging, exciting even, and with an hour still to go, I decided to push the boat a little further out. There was no shortage of pigs in the market and I bought twenty from one of the other firms who were so pleased to see the back of them, they were weighed, loaded, and delivered to my stall almost before I returned there myself. I should perhaps mention that although competition between rival firms was always extremely keen (cut-throat is the right term) inter-trading such as I've just described was quite common. At the time I thought I could spend the remaining hour splitting the pigs in readiness for next day, but what really happened was that as fast as I could split them, I was asked for legs or loins or whatever and by closing time they had all gone and I was sold out once again. There was no doubting that, for all the wrong reasons, I'd hit on something, and this without a single comment to (or from) my dad.

That weekend I was busy. With Big Bill as assistant and timber from the local yard I manufactured a display stand with three shelves and also a stand for a butcher's chopping block, complete even with a drawer for tools. By the end of that week my new pig-selling caper was building up nicely, and another week later saw me selling a massive two hundred pigs a week; which turned out to be the maximum because, what with the lambs and calves, we had no room to hang more. Beef, of course, was always our main product, not only in numbers but in profitability, and took up every inch of hanging space in the other two stalls.

That was what became of probably the only serious row I ever had with my dad. I became a pork salesman and cutter, handling two hundred pigs a week almost regularly throughout the year and very nice too. There was sadness in it just the same, because the business with that lamb salesman stuck in my head and I never did manage to shake it out – the ability to forgive and forget (or rather the lack of it) is something else I seem to have inherited from that father of mine. The lamb salesman himself incidentally was no great shakes at the job and didn't stay with us very long, although the one who took his place was a splendid chap, which is just as well. I had no intention of going back there again, and I don't mean that in a spiteful way. The fact was that the pork selling suited me better. I'm active by nature, and although the lamb-selling was something of a challenge, the actual work involved in the pork job took some of the boredom away – job-satisfaction they call it. The faster and more skilled I became the better I liked it, and the satisfaction went even further. This pork-selling thing was entirely my own doing, with no-one telling me to do it or even showing me how. The first business venture I had tackled entirely on my own. It's a bit like my army service. The reason I've always been proud of the fact that I made the rank of Staff-Sergeant is because my dad could never claim to have helped me do it.

Now although everything I have written is absolutely true in word and implication, in one respect it's a half-truth, and that won't do. Where one specific cause of friction between Shutkever Junior and Senior was concerned, he was entirely in the right and I entirely in the wrong. The tragedy is that it took me years to realise it, by which time my dad was gone.

Quite often in a jocular vein, although with a definite seriousness as well, my dad would point out how much more profitable were the cattle he bought compared with my efforts, and our system was such that every single beast was kept separate as far as records were concerned. There was no guessing about it – it was a fact. After one such session, I got worked up to the extent that, in the office and in front of the staff, I put it to him straight by asking why, if I was such a dead loss as both buyer and salesman, he made so much fuss when I went on holiday? It was a bit below the belt because he hated holidays himself, and had never taken one. Nevertheless, it stumped him which was a rare enough occurrence in itself. Then came a time when I was worked-up enough to put my finger on what I considered the nub of the argument.

'What chance have my poor old bullocks got?' I asked, with another of his comparison complaints well on the build. 'You only kill my stuff when trade's bad. Saturday's kill and all the respectable order trade you reserve for your own.' Let's not get confused over this. We were, by now, full partners and the actual ownership was not under discussion: 'His' and 'Mine' meant no more than who purchased them. My accusation was absolutely sound and what's more my dad didn't even try to deny it.

'What else can I do? The rubbish you bring home would lose us every customer we've got.'

'Bullshit,' I said. We never minced matters, either of us.

But I'm afraid my dad was right, and I can't leave this topic without saying so. The truth was that I only thought I understood meat. I knew enough to hold my own against yobs, like Harry Wooton under the old system, but that, I'm sorry to say, was not enough. When it came to judging quality of meat to the standard required to satisfy Louis Shutkever's customers, it was a different story. It was only after my dad died, and I took over the beef stall, that I found out. Also I must say, it's not a scrap of use my trying to blame my dad for not showing me the job properly in the first place, because that's something else I have since discovered.

There are things that can be taught and things that can't. Some things have to come by themselves or they never come at all.

Chapter Twenty-One

Monk & Co.

•

G H Monk & Co was a meat wholesale business in Birmingham Market, and for all I know, had been there since the place opened. It was a size-able outfit with branches in at least one other town. Old-established, but still seeking expansion so that it could be said it was old-fashioned and forward-looking at the same time. The name of G H Monk had been a background noise for as long as I can remember. They were important in more ways than one, so although I decided from the first to leave other firms out of this account, I am going to make an exception in their hon-our (if that's the right word). The truth is that George Henry Monk who, if not the founder, was certainly the mainstay of the company, played much the same part in my dad's life as did Harry Wooton in mine. So although it was many years before my time, back with the Lloyd George's and the suffragettes, constant repetition has hammered the story in so deep as to be virtually word perfect. And when, on that first Monday morning, I found a few seconds to look away from my rows of lambs, I couldn't help but see the name of G H Monk almost everywhere It was glaring down at me from ten-foot long boards, hung above the next five stalls to my right and two directly opposite – our next door neighbours for the next twenty years.

I never met George Monk, although he was still about at the time we re-opened the business, still living in Birmingham and on our side of the city at that. By all accounts he was a thick-set, smart-looking man, more cunning than clever (I'm told), and something of a hard-head. That last bit doesn't surprise me much. I can't call to mind a single person who ever made a bag of beans in the meat business that was anything else. He was never to know it, but my earliest recollections of life and my original entry into the meat business had to do with Monk & Co (laughable really, because it was around 1934 when I was seven) but just the same, I think that's where I'll start.

Our old farmhouse roof had been in a bad way for years and a windy night usually meant there'd be a smashed tile or two lying about the yard next morning. The sparrows had known about all this for a long time and used the cracks and spaces as a means of entrance to their nesting sites between the rafters. So when I was awakened, early one Saturday morning, I put it down to the racket in the roof, a common occurrence at nesting time. I was wrong once again. It wasn't coming from the roof but from the window, and would have sounded like heavy raindrops had it been more regula. Also, and more to the point, it wasn't raining. There it went again, 'tap', it went, 'taptap – taptap'. Out of bed and at the window and the mystery was solved. Down below, standing in the yard, was Jim Cook. In his left hand a load of gravel pebbles, in his right a single one he was about to throw, and in mid-air, another that arrived at the glass at the same time as I did. On seeing me Jim dropped the remainder of the ammunition and beckoned me down. There was a load of cattle at the railway station and if I got myself dressed a bit sharpish, I could go with him and help drive them home. Incidentally, I would like to emphasise that 'if I was quick enough I could,' should not be confused with, 'would I go with him?' or (God forbid) 'I'll give you a shilling if you'll come.' Jim Cook was doing me a favour by getting me out of bed and allowing me to help drive a load of cattle the four miles from the local railway station. What's more, I must have agreed with him because I was still tucking my shirt in after I'd mounted my bike and chased him up our driveway. No allowance for age or size whatever. I'll spare the details of this enjoyable caper that was to occur quite regularly around that time, except to say that although we went to great trouble to ensure all gates were closed on the way there, by the time we were on the trail back, there were always a few who'd thought fit to open them again. In this way several well-kept lawns and gardens were stampeded over from time to time, although there never was chance or thought for apologies so it didn't really spoil the fun. Now what (you may well ask) has this to do with G H Monk & Co of City Meat Market, Birmingham? Well, I'll tell you.

It was none other than George Monk himself who tried to upset my dad's applecart at pre-war Barnt Green by warning the auctioneer about Shutkever's lack of finance, which resulted, if you remember, in the bag-of-sixpences' affair. Partly through normal business jealousy, partly through sheer bloody-mindedness, and partly through prejudice against foreigners and especially Jews (which I'm sorry to say was rampant in the meat business of those times), there were men wishing to see the back of Louis Shutkever, and the most persistent of them all was George Monk. It was much the same as my stack-up with Harry Wooton a generation later, except that in those days the methods were different. With road transport of cattle in its infancy and cattle lorries still something of a novelty, it was a simple matter for a large outfit like Monk & Co to intimidate the transporters at Banbury into refusing to work for Shutkever, leaving no alternative but to use the railway. It wasn't a serious problem. In fact, the railway was actually cheaper. I certainly enjoyed the job and don't think Jim Cook minded it too much. The trouble was the time delay and also the distress factor to the animals, necessitating a few days rest period before they could be killed. In short, the whole thing was a bloody nuisance, and G H Monk, our new neighbour, was the sole cause of it.

For the really bad blood that ran between the two men I have to rely on my dad's version of what happened much later. It might be completely true, it might be half true, and it might be a little distorted, although I've no reason to doubt that my dad himself considered it one hundred per-cent true and the facts and results seem to bear him out. When the Ministry of Food took over the meat business, somebody who knew what he was about was needed to run places like Birmingham Abattoir and as head of the biggest firm in the market, George Monk clicked for that very key job. In the early days of the war the meat business was considered important enough for its workforce to come under the 'reserved occupa-tion' category, and were consequently not called up for military service. But as the war crept on, the net was tightened with ever more men being taken off the reserve list. Now my dad has always insisted that Monk used his influence to ensure that his own men stayed, while regardless of skill or anything else, other firms' men were released.

I've never tried to prove or disprove this theory and wouldn't know how to, but when I take into account George Monk's reputation (among friend and foe alike) for far-sightedness and downright cunning, I can't look away from the fact that it was probably so. Just the same, it would have been no more than a touch of opportunism or business tactics and probably forgotten year's ago, except for the fact my dad's slaughterhouse foreman (Old Harry's son) was among those allowed to go and was killed at Anzio. Naturally enough, neither my dad, nor Old Harry, were ever to forgive George Monk for what they considered as his part in it.

The outcome of all this was that right from the first day the Shutkever/Monk war, that had lain dormant for fourteen years, came back to life and this, despite the fact that Monk himself had long since dropped out of the picture and his next in line inherited it, so to speak. They came face to face every Tuesday at Stratford Market and the fur and feathers flew week after week. I thought it was a bit silly, although the name of Monk & Co had been dirty words in my dad's book for so long I knew it more than my life was worth to say as much. To me (and I could be wrong) it was similar to the present day Irish situation and had gone on for so long that the combatants had forgotten how or even why it started. If so, all I can say is I hope they both end in the same way.

There came a day when, after a long drawn-out heatwave that had left us all gasping and meat almost un-sellable, we had stood in the market morning after morning and hardly glimpsed a butcher for days. (When a shop butcher talks of good weather, he means the brass-monkey variety.) We went to Stratford Market on the Tuesday, leaving behind a stall full of meat, a lairage full of cattle and a farm packed to capacity; not wanting a single bullock or even 'a hair off one', as my dad used to say. And Monk & Co, and every other wholesaler from Land's End upwards, must have felt exactly the same. The strange thing is that it would never have occurred to any of us to take a day off and not go. We all took our places by the ringside and waited for the bell, same as ever. Such times are depressing for everybody; farmers, buyers, and especially the poor old auctioneers, working themselves into a lather trying to coax the un-coaxable. Yet even though absolutely nothing is wanted, sooner or later a bid gets put in just to break the monotony.

A beautiful bullock that would have taken a first prize in any cattle show came ambling into the ring shortly after the start, and my old dad just couldn't resist it. He sang out a bid, loud enough to startle the starlings in the rafters, although I can't remember what it was and it doesn't matter anyway. What does matter is that the boss of G H Monk & Co, standing where he always stood, about four places to our left, looked at the bullock, then directly at my dad, and didn't bid a single shilling. Now that was mighty strange in spite of everything, and it got stranger still as the day went by, because they bought a load of cattle each, absolutely dirt cheap, and without once bidding on each other. I must say again that neither of them wanted any cattle at all, but that doesn't alter things a scrap because cattlemen don't live by normal rules. In fact, they're a funny lot altogether.

Heatwave or not, I knew, my dad knew, and anyone with any knowledge of the politics of Birmingham Meat Market knew, that something very odd had happened at Stratford that day. Any lingering doubt that might have remained was cleared up once and for all the following morning. The boss of Monk & Co, Arthur Ashley, came on our stall, which meant walking a full twenty feet from where he usually stood (although metaphorically a million miles), gave my dad a cigar, and those two old warriors shook hands and remained friends thereafter. As I said earlier, the Irish problem, the Russian problem, the Arab/Jew problem and all the rest could no doubt be settled almost as easily but, of course, they never will.

That sounds like the end of that tale, but in fact, it isn't because around that time another aspect, totally unexpected and somewhat mind-bending occurred. I remember it quite clearly, and the way it stunned my dad, although I'm not sure exactly when it was.

A few hundred yards down the road and around the corner from Birmingham Market was a paper shop (wrapping – not news) and above it, up those two very steep stairs with no handrail mentioned in the Big Tom-and-the-safe episode, was our office. It was a left-over from before the war, as dull and dingy as the stairs that led to it, but with so low a rent that my dad had kept it on all through the years and did his paperwork from there. I never stayed up there a moment longer than necessary because I'm not much for office work at the best of times, but every Saturday after the market closed (10 o'clock) we assembled there to go through the week's business, pay the bills (every week, my dad reckoned to owe nothing to nobody), and anything else that came up.

On the Saturday in question, we were all finished and about to go home when the telephone rang. None other than G H Monk himself – my dad's all-time bogey man. Had I known who it was and what he wanted, believe me I'd have stayed where I was. But as it was, my dad, who answered the phone and was too stunned to say anything, or else I didn't give him the chance, with things to do back home I dived off and left him to it.

G H Monk (always referred to as such – initials and name) was by then an old man and had been seriously ill for some time. Now, suddenly and out of the blue, came his phone call. He wanted to come to the office and speak to my dad. He did just that, that same day, and had to drag his poor old bones up those two flights of cranky old stairs to do it. I've already said the thing left my dad stunned, and there's no other word for it. He never did tell me how long the man stayed or what they talked about although they shook hands, which seemed to be the main reason for the visit. Two week's later, G H Monk was dead, and I've always been sorry I missed that chance to meet him, although I can't think why because I'd hated the man (by proxy) all my life.

There is a further sequence to this chapter which I might as well include at this point, although it's a big dive forward in time and took place in late 1960. By that time the set-up had changed yet again, and as far as Shutkever & Son was concerned, not for the better (and foisted on us without option). It came about by a change in the laws governing the slaughtering of animals and the key part was to do with cruelty and its elimination. Under the new scheme it was forbidden for one animal to be able to see another being killed. I'm not too sure that it was soundly based. Animals are stressed the moment they leave their home farm, however carefully handled. Certainly being herded together with strange bedfellows in the totally alien atmosphere of both cattle market and abattoir, with all the unusual noises and smells, must increase the torment to such degree that seeing other animals killed a moment before oblivion seems to me a very small consideration. I've been wrong before and probably am now, but in any case I've no complaint to make. Anything that might alleviate animal suffering is all right by me. It was the outcome that was bad. There was no room in our abattoir to construct separate stunning pens and after long and protracted negotiations, both among ourselves and the Markets and Fairs Committee, we were finally saddled with a very expensive solution. At a cost of £83,000 to be found out of increased rent, a new and mechanical slaughtering system was to be installed, and the extra cost, as far as we were concerned, was the best part. In order to work this new system, the slaughtermen were to be drafted into a separate company and kill for everybody – which lost us the Tricklebanks, our pride and joy.

This new outfit was, by design, a non-profit making service company and in order to see fair play, each firm appointed its own representative on the board. In our case it was me, and in the case of G H Monk, it was Arthur Ashley. We met once a month to discuss general items and once a year we got together for the AGM, a bit on the prim and proper side, although friendly enough, with a respectable dinner and plenty of free drink thrown in for luck. Arthur Ashley's car had broken down some months before (a broken fan belt) and, as it happened, I was not only on the spot, but able to dash round the corner to a firm I knew, get him a new belt, and finish the job by crawling about (in a fine summer shower) to put it on. Arthur never forgot this, told everybody about it and I seem to have made a pal for life, although to be sure, I'd have done the same for anybody (except perhaps Harry Wooton and a few other unmentionables). Anyway, to get back to where we were, what with the chance of a few free drinks, and Arthur being a nervous sort of chap, he asked me if I'd give him a lift to the AGM which I did quite gladly. It was a long ride home because Arthur lived a good ten miles further out of town than I did. We were both nicely happy (without being in any way intoxicated, I must insist) and in the mood to talk. As can be expected, it started off with a few of Arthur's anecdotes, all about cattle buying and involving himself and my dad, and all years before my time.

It appeared that it was not uncommon for them to go round the farms together on buying expeditions, which culminated in the tossing of coins to see who got the spoils. It all sounded a bit hairy, to say the least, although I'm quite sure he was telling the truth. Yet the more I heard, the more puzzled I became until eventually, I had to stop him.

'Tell me something, Arthur.' I jumped in the moment he stopped for breath. 'There's something bothering me about all this. All my life, man and boy, I've been brought up on the belief that G H Monk was a dirty word, yet from what you've just said you all seem to have been best of pals – what went wrong?' Arthur stopped and stared, looked away and then back again, and was quiet for so long, I thought I'd stopped him for good.

'To tell you the truth, I don't know myself,' was the final analysis. 'It was a long time ago and I was only a very junior director at the time. Whatever happened was between George Monk and your dad – nothing to do with me.' Which was all I was to get on the subject, then or after. What's more, it sobered me up enough to spoil what had been a very pleasant journey, so I wished I hadn't bothered. Afterwards, however, I got to thinking about it, and what I came up with is worth writing, if only because it's a good pointer to the kind of idiocy that goes into the making of cattlemen. Without wishing to be unkind to Arthur Ashley, who not only liked me but proved it, by getting me out of trouble on more than one occasion. I'd describe him as a mild, easy-going type of man, not self-made and certainly neither as hard nor as clever as my dad or the other meat men I've written about. I'd say he got to where he was by long service to his company and very little else. Yet he had picked up and carried on a fight that must have cost his firm hundreds, thousands even, without knowing (if he was telling me the truth) what it was all about. And even if he was the one who actually called it off, it was exactly as I've described – a pure accident.

Stratford Christmas Fatstock show and sale – 1964.

On the right with the stick is Mr Barnard, auctioneer. In the middle
with the bowler is Arthur Ashley – boss of G H Monks & Co.
On the extreme left is the camera-shy Louis Shutkever.

Chapter Twenty-Two

Back to the Future

•

At Christmas 1973, I finally closed down my wholesale meat enterprise and, by so doing turned my back on everything my dad had worked a hard lifetime to establish. It was a sad end to a grand struggle, but I can't hold myself to blame, as there was little I could do about it. Along with all the other fresh-meat tenants of Birmingham Market, we had been planned out of existence, and although one or two others did attempt to hang on, to the best of my knowledge, they have all gone now. There is no way to set out just what happened to us all without delving into local and national politics, although that was never my intention.

What happened was that, for reasons with which I still can't come to terms, Birmingham City Council decided that in the name of progress and part of a massive redevelopment scheme, the meat market was to be demolished and replaced by a new, modern, concrete and steel market complex, along with the fish, fruit and vegetables. All in the one great glorious conglomerate. We didn't need telling what that would mean. Vastly increased rents for a start, but the real bogey was that that was only the start. There was far worse to come. In the new market all we were to get for our rent was a bare space, no rails, refrigerators, or furniture of any kind which, even way back in the seventies, meant crawling to the banks for loans. A thing my dear old dad had never believed in.

It really started some years before with that new killing law I've described and the changes it brought about, and although I can't speak for everybody, I'm sure the large percentage of fresh-meat firms in our market were happy with things as they were. However, the Markets and Fairs Dept were adamant – if we didn't agree to the changes envisaged we would lose our slaughtering facilities altogether, not just for now, but for the new market complex (which we didn't want either). We had meetings galore, all of which seemed a waste of time then, and have proved so ever since. Only one man on the council side (a retired railway man if I remember rightly) was willing to listen to the views of men with lifetime experience in the meat trade. All the rest were like a brick wall, just as solid and, I'm sorry to say, every bit as thick. The pack-leader had the gall to tell us, point blank, that slaughtering was a dirty trade and he didn't want it in his city. From a practical viewpoint, however, their main plank appeared to be that the foundations of the old market were crumbling away. If they mentioned it once, we heard it a thousand times and I still don't believe it. Man had not yet walked on the moon it's true, but the atom had been split, antibiotics had arrived, and I'm sure we'd reached the point where a ton or two of concrete could be pumped into place, a lot cheaper than what finally materialized. In any case the old market was built like a fortress. They then backed-up this foundation nonsense by bringing in the parking problem, which I freely admit as a valid debating point. Although, when I now make my rare visits to the new market, at busy times it's no improvement on the old. Even so, had they limited their argument to just butcher's vans they would have been on fairly safe ground, but they strayed off to include – emphasise even – the traffic chaos caused by the cattle transporters' wagons, and here they were on very rocky terrain indeed.

Cattle lorries in those days held about twelve bullocks to the load, and a driver could back up, unload his cattle, hand them over to the market drover and be on his way in fifteen minutes without hurrying. In the new set-up (as we repeatedly tried to point out) those same twelve bullocks would arrive killed and dressed and converted into forty-eight quarters of beef, plus the attendant offal. All of which would need to be man-handled off the transports and hung on the stalls, an hour's work for two men plus the lorry driver. And all that time, the meat lorry, bigger and bulkier than a cattle truck, would be standing and occupying valuable space. It made no difference – nobody listened.

When it became apparent that the battle was lost, I got desperate enough to go solo, which didn't do any good, but I'm still glad I tried. I approached the Housewives League, the Farmer's Union, then (accompanied by the chairman of the slaughtering company), journeyed to the Houses of Parliament and laid it on our Member, but although there were some friendly noises here and there, I don't really think anybody knew what we were talking about. The sad outcome is that although we now have a new city centre that some find an improvement, from a meat point of view, everybody has lost. There are no killing facilities in today's Birmingham Meat Market. The meat for this city is now hauled in from God knows where, already dead, not as fresh as it should be and handled many times on and off transports, which doesn't make it any cleaner. As for the butchers, their choice is lessened to a degree bordering on the old wartime standards, whereby they have to make do with what can be found. The school for inspectors has gone, an old-established training ground for slaughtermen has disappeared, and the poor old farmers have lost a well-run casualty department which was a boon in time of serious trouble and certainly an improvement on the alternative – the knacker-man.

Having said all that, before I move on, I would like to make one thing abundantly clear once and for all. This is not a case of sour grapes. I have not been kicked out of anywhere, but merely crossed the river, and for many years now I've been working this farm and producing beef for some other poor devil to sell. The only difference is that instead of getting up at five-thirty in the morning and racing to Birmingham Market whilst all decent folk are still abed, I take my cattle to Banbury, have a good dinner in their excellent dining room, and with any luck at all, manage to squeeze a sort of living out of it. A happy man in fact.

Just the same I think, after all these years, I can look at what has become of the meat business, from a distance as it were, and to be honest, I don't like what I see. The story of Birmingham Market seems to be happening all over. Abattoirs are closing, firms are disappearing almost every week, and it all points to a monopoly situation which can only spell misery for farmer, butcher, and housewife alike. Worse still, nobody seems to care. No doubt it will sort itself out somehow, but if there is a silver lining it seems to be hiding a long way back. Then there's this anti-meat attitude which appears to be foisted on the public by today's media. Not just meat but milk, butter, everything the farmer produces has suddenly become positively deadly. I don't know whether Lord Bob has explained the situation to them or not, but if he has, those poor Ethiopians must think we've all fallen off our perches.

We come now to my last trick, and it calls for some daring, and not a little stealth. The windows in this old farmhouse are all double-glazed, and with the price of glass these days, I fear for the future. Nevertheless I must broach the wretched subject of the Animal Rights Brigade, because I honestly don't know what makes them tick, at least from a meat point of view. Medical experimentation is another matter and best left alone, because I know nothing about it.

I am a countryman born and bred, have always enjoyed it and earned a living out of it so I'm not just a countryman but a professional countryman. Be they wild or domesticated, mine or anyone else's, I love all animals, birds, trees, hills, skies, blue for preference; I love them all. On my land there are hares, pheasants, partridges, Canada geese, foxes, the whole kaleidoscope. I get great pleasure out of watching them and, Heaven forbid I should ever get hungry enough to want to eat a single one. I admit only to the poisoning of rats, but it's done out of sheer necessity, and I certainly derive no pleasure from it. When it comes to killing animals for meat, however, I see nothing wrong or cruel in it whatever, and what's more, I can see no alternative.

Our nutritionists tell us we could live on soya beans and such and who am I to argue with them? No doubt we could manage without leather although much the poorer for it, then there's milk; could we manage without milk? Because if we can't, the calves must die – we can't both have it. And if, out of kindness, we don't kill the calves, what will become of them? Should they be left to die of old age under the hedges? Or perhaps become weak enough for other animals to kill them? Do we want a land where dead and rotting carcasses are lying everywhere? Short of reintroducing wolves, and establishing some sizable broods of vultures, that's what we'd have. And anyone who thinks slaughtering in an abattoir is cruel, should watch how animals and birds go about it. Kestrels, beautiful as they are, sit on telephone poles and tear mice to pieces while they're still alive! It's horrific! I could go on ad nauseam because I've thought about such things for hours – some farm-work is monotonous to the extent that if the mind wasn't allowed to wander we would all go barmy. All I'm trying to say is that if those self-appointed guardians of all God's creatures were to sit down and think things over, it might have a calming influence.

In the meantime, I get great comfort from looking out of my window at an oak tree in my orchard hedge. It has stood there for over a hundred years, and with any luck will be there for the next hundred.

Epilogue

•

I wrote this account whilst on light duties, convalescing from a back operation some twenty-five years ago. Backache, by the way, is a well-known by-product of farming. My health is now in a much better state but I am sorry to report that the same cannot be said for either the meat trade or the farming industry. Despite all our best endeavours, the old meat traders failed to convince the Markets and Fairs Committee of the folly of their grandiose plans and unfortunately all our gloomiest predictions have come true. So, with many of my friends and 'tame readers' nagging me to bring my account up to date, I've decided to give it a try. But a word of warning. My natural optimism is going to be stretched to the limit if I'm not to produce a truly depressing account.

To take up the tale where it left off, I closed my butchering business at Christmas 1973, and since then have had no direct connection with the meat trade as such. I do however make the occasional visit to the new market to chat with a few ancient remnants (but mainly to find something to eat). For anyone brought up in the old tradition, the meat trade in Birmingham and the building in which it's housed is really a most depressing sight. Even the freshest of meat on show looks a bit woebegone by our standards, which would be no surprise to anyone from the old school and really only to be expected. Our cattle were brought in and rested, expertly killed and dressed on the premises, then hung to cool and set in that grand old sales hall that was our home for over thirty years. Today's meat is killed elsewhere, mauled on and off lorries and carted for miles, to be then handled several times again before the butchers get their first look at it. That is not saying that there is anything wrong with it. It is all refrigerated and, no doubt, perfectly sound but all that shunting about certainly does nothing to improve the looks of it. The only conclusion to be drawn is that our old shop butchers must have lowered their standards several degrees since my time, or given up the ghost and retired.

This might sound like a nostalgic old dodger decrying everything modern (which in fact I usually do), but there is another way to compare the lamentable decline in Birmingham's wholesale meat situation since our day. Shutkever and Son started out in 1954 with two stalls in the old market, and had to fight to get even them. It was a full three years before another stall came our way, and then only due to the voluntary liquidation of another trader. In today's 'new' market there are already several stalls locked and shuttered and the general feeling is that there will soon be more to follow. Of the few men remaining from the old market, many are only awaiting pension day and clinging to the hope that the market itself will stay the course. If there is a happy person anywhere in the place, master or man, I've yet to find him.

Without the live cattle aspect and the slaughtering side, all the hustle and bustle has gone, adding several degrees to the gloom that hangs over the place like a shroud. Truth to tell, I usually make my visit on a Wednesday, which always was the quietest day of the week, but that's no excuse. In the old place there was more action to be found on a Sunday morning. The only improvement I've found up to now has nothing to do with the council's planning or, in fact, the meat trade at all. Decimalisation has ushered in a host of little gadgets called calculators and as I watch them flashing and clicking like demented fireworks, I wonder just how today's sales clerks would have coped with those dreadful carbon copies and greasy biro's with which we fought a losing fight every day. Electronic scales now flash up a mine of information, although there is no way of knowing just how accurate any of it is. They could be linked direct to the main offices (wherever they are) and doing away with a few dozen clerical jobs, which I know, for certain, my old dad would have lost little sleep over.

There is still an army of inspectors walking about, but the miners' lamps have gone and nowadays they sport white coats rather than the old khaki, topped off with gleaming white crash helmets, more in keeping with American speed cops. Without any slaughtering facilities, today's inspectors must be hard pressed filling their days. They do keep a sharp eye out for anyone reckless enough to light a cigarette and there's always the odd bully-beef tin with a dent or two, but with all the meat coming into the market having already passed inspection at the abattoirs where it was killed, the poor devils must worry about redundancy from time to time. I suppose over-inspection is better than no inspection at all, except that it's charged to the wholesaler, so the consumer gets saddled with the cost sooner or later.

There is no getting away from the fact that where meat is concerned, the citizens of Birmingham and surrounding districts have been very badly served indeed. A city of this size and importance should be in direct charge of its own meat inspection and have its own slaughtering facilities, rather than having to rely on others. The meat men of our day were well-known and respected wherever they went, for the keenness of their buyers and the very high quality always insisted on, and if Birmingham councillors didn't appreciate them, other towns and cities most certainly did. The moment Coventry and Derby saw what was happening, we were offered space in their abattoirs and sales halls and, in fact, at one time, the move was given serious consideration. But disruptions of that nature are really only for 20 and 30 year-olds, so like a lot of other schemes nothing came of it.

I hope all that has not proved too depressing, because I now come to the BSE fiasco and believe me, BSE makes all the rest look like a holiday in the sun.

I think it was some time in the late 1980s that we first heard about Mad Cow Disease. We saw that black-and-white cow sliding and staggering about and heard various experts telling us what they thought about it. For a long time it was believed that only pedigree Friesian cows were susceptible and that beef breeds were unaffected. Strangely enough, it always seems to be dairy cows we see on telly (usually that same one) so although I don't actually know, it would seem that beef breeds are less involved (that could be wrong of course). Just the same, it is fairly safe to say that it was in the dairy section that something went badly wrong.

That doesn't give the media the right to point their mischievous fingers at farmers willy-nilly with tales of greed, because I maintain that even if it was dangerous animal food that caused the problem, the farmers were more victims than villains. Like everyone else in business they were looking to keep their costs down, and when offered that reconstituted feed, passed by all the experts as OK, and not warned about by the government or anyone else, they gave it a try. After the event, the scientific bodies who (I think) were as much to blame as anyone, then tried to get the government to finance an inquiry into the matter to the tune of £3million. The government jibbed, and at that stage with just a handful of sick cows to go on, thought that the professors were out to feather their nests (not unknown). We all know now just how serious the situation was and the debate goes on, but in the meantime what's going to happen to the farmers?

To our friends across the Channel this was a wonderful chance to ruin our agricultural industry and they were exceedingly quick to capitalise on the situation. At the drop of a hat, they got together to deplore the dangers and forbade not just their own people, but the whole world, from eating our beef. It didn't matter that they had been importing our cattle for years or that they had been feeding the same dodgy food to their animals for as long as we have, and went on using it long after we had stopped. So it's a dead certainty that there is Mad Cow Disease over there, although they hide it. The real tragedy is that the Conservative Government laid down and died, allowing our good neighbours to walk all over us and up to now, the present lot are doing no better.

All our affected farms were sealed off and a large-scale slaughtering and burning orgy was put into action that still goes on. As a first step, all feedstuff that was considered the cause was withdrawn and destroyed. It was then decided, that as there must be other animals that had eaten the food but were not yet known to be infected, as a further safeguard, all cattle over thirty months of age were barred from the food chain. Now that was very strong medicine for the farmers to swallow, but on the old principle that desperate ills call for desperate remedies, it was accepted. What we didn't realise, and still can't come to terms with, is that the Over Thirty Month Rule is still being applied today (3rd August 2005). Seventeen years after the last of the infected food has been destroyed! It is unreasonable, unnecessary, ridiculous and purely political, with no bearing on health at all. And it's costing the farmers a fortune. Even some Germans have been known to say that it's crazy.

The BSE epidemic is beginning to fade, but it was followed almost immediately by a wide spread outbreak of Foot and Mouth Disease, and together they have left us with a raft of rules and regulations that are doing far more damage than the diseases themselves. We are continually being bombarded with multi-coloured, glossy-paged and expensively produced brochures, some of which run to twenty or thirty pages. There are dozens of baffling questions to be answered and little boxes galore, all needing to be ticked or crossed correctly. And woe betide anyone who makes, or crosses out, a mistake. Back come all the same forms, usually accompanied by threats of dire financial punishments, reminders of time limits, court cases, or worse. It would seem that DEFRA (which is just another name for the Min. of Ag.) considers that livestock farmers are a cross between naughty children and downright thieves.

By far the worst and most damaging of these directives, however, is that 'Over Thirty Months Scheme' (OTMS). It has already proved too much for hundreds of dairy farmers who have given up, with many more sure to follow, and it makes matters no better to be told that the scheme itself was never based on any actual health or safety considerations.

Having stated, loudly and often, that BSE was caused by feeding bovine animals on re-constituted food (a claim still being debated), the vets and scientists have dug themselves into a bunker. With all the early affected cattle being old milking cows, and unable to ban meat eating completely, they needed a cut-off point, after which meat was considered unsafe to eat. Back they went to that old 'cow-heifer' criteria of yesteryear. Thirty months is the age at which bovine animals lose the last of their calf teeth, making it a recognisable point, which was the sole reason thirty months of age was the chosen cut-off point. And that was seventeen years ago!

Today, all our cattle have passports, which state their place of birth, all movements since, and most important of all, date of birth. This changes the whole situation. A cut-off point could now be established almost anywhere, making the thirty month rule as ancient as chain-mail. In that seventeen-year period, hundreds of tons of perfectly sound meat has been wasted; not only a loss to the farmer, but a drain on the government who must pay the compensation. These are by no means trivial amounts. The value lost to the exchequer to date would have supplied all the hospitals and schools needed for a generation. And it still goes on. It's bad enough for beef producers like me, because any animal approaching that dreaded thirty months must be rushed off to market, ready or not, and even if only one day over, no auction or abattoir can accept them. They go to be burned.

For the milk producer, never blessed with a decent profit margin at the best of times, it is even worse. Dairy farmers have always relied to some extent on the sale of old cows that were past their working life, 'culls' they are called. But with all such animals being way past the thirty months age limit, they all must go to the crematorium. The farmers are compensated, but as with all government payouts, it rarely represents the cows' real value, and never the cost of replacements.

Less serious, but another expensive nuisance is the Farm Assurance Scheme. To join FABBL (Farm Assured British Beef and Lamb) costs nearly £100 each year. First an inspector comes to see the farm and studies all your collection of paperwork. He looks at your cattle movement records and checks them against your cattle passports, looks at your dog's passport, wants to know if you've wormed your cattle, how long ago? And what with? Next comes his brochure, listing all the things you must, and must not do, and believe me, there is nothing in that document that any farmer has not been doing all his working life. He even told me that I couldn't spread muck on the fields where the cows graze, but when I pointed out that the cows mucked on the fields all the time, he moved on to other things. Once accepted, you get a plaque to stick on the farm gate, and at market, your cattle have special tickets stuck on their backs to tell buyers from the supermarkets that your animals are from a FABBL registered farm. The supermarkets are kidded into thinking that there is something special about them, when in fact there isn't. At the same time, the auctioneers also make a point of telling us that, without the super-market buyers, they have difficulty making top price for cattle without those FABBL tickets. So the trick has two edges to it. It's a sort of gov-ernment-sponsored blackmail. A stealth tax in fact.

Throughout this account, I have tried to show the important part that the knackerman always played in livestock marketing. As I've said, knackermen were a bit like football referees. Nobody loved them but they couldn't be done without. Unfortunately, in the name of disease-preven-tion, the knackermeat business has now been hygienically emaciated to the point of extinction, and the few operators left, that were an asset in time of trouble, have now become a serious expense. Dead animals should have value. Their carcasses, hides, bones etc., that were once marketable commodities, have now been converted into tons of dead-weight refuse. Carting this rubbish away is a costly business and all to be passed back to the farmer, at about £80 per cow.

Human nature being what it is, dead animals began to be found dumped in rivers and woods, which was hardly what the government had in mind. So now we have the Fallen Stock Scheme. For a yearly sub-scription, DEFRA undertakes the removal of all our dead animals. It's a sort of insurance we must take out, even if all our animals are alive and well, and I'm told that, due mainly to long delays in the actual collec-tions, up until now it has not been working too well.

The rundown of all branches of livestock farming is now an established fact, and the signs are there for all to see. All that remains of Stratford Market, my dad's favourite, are a few concrete oblongs where the cattle yards used to be, and even Banbury, the largest cattle market in Europe, folded two or three years ago. Banbury Market was a colossal business with a turnover in the millions, and attracted buyers from all over Europe. One operator even had several farms and a ship of his own, all standing by to cope with the hundreds of sheep and cattle collected every Thursday at Banbury. The export ban has put paid to all that, and in so doing has ren-dered the OTMS even more ridiculous. The government was naive enough to think that the OTMS would force the Continentals – namely the French, to relax their politically motivated ban – some hope!

The advent of supermarkets has had a monumental affect in the shap-ing of today's agricultural situation, and having done away with almost everything resembling opposition, they are now beginning to gobble up each other. Creeping monopolistic developments of that nature rarely benefit the consumer in the long run, and are already having a devastating effect on the producers. It doesn't look good. So strong has supermarket buying-power become that (if reputed news reports are to be believed) negotiated contracts are often scrapped without warning. When special offers are announced as daily goodwill gestures to the housewife, the shoppers are delighted; my own wife regularly dives in for them, but nobody is told that the farmer's contracted and agreed payment is then reduced to cover the cost. What can a producer do when forty or fifty acres of cabbage that is already growing in his field, is suddenly and seriously devalued owing to a change in company policy? We thought trading situations were tough in the old days, and they were, but at least there was an element of British fair play. A hand-shake in those days was worth something, and certainly worth more than many of today's written contracts, no matter how many solicitors have underwritten them. I am continually being reminded of my dad's views on the subject: 'If a man's word is no good, his signature is no better.'

It doesn't look good.

Advancing old age, however, has lifted me above most of this misery, because although I am still a farmer, with cattle to feed and markets to attend, it is now on such a scale that I have more time to enjoy it. Also, due to a happening that occurred over twenty years ago, I have partially re-captured some of a long-lost youth.

On leaving the local post office, sometime in the late 1980s, I bumped into Jim Cook, white haired and long retired by then, but still sprightly and upright in his walk. At the time I had a few cattle grazing on a pal's field in the next village. I was on my way to feed them some hay, and on the spur of the moment, I invited Jim to come along for the ride. As anyone who has ever looked after animals will agree, it is by far the most satisfying part of farming, and that day, working along with Jim again, it was like a return to the good old days. Every move he made told me that he had missed farming since leaving us, and although it's difficult to explain, there is a right way of doing every little thing in farming. I could tell by the way he shook out the hay, the way he placed it close to the hedgerow to minimise the chance of the cattle treading on it, and the way he walked round looking the animals over that old Jim was back in his kingdom. It was the start of a new routine.

From then on, whenever there was any cattle work to do, I called Jim in, and he never needed calling twice. He was still good with animals, a real help, and it would have been difficult to decide which of us enjoyed the company most. There was never a mention of payment because I knew it would annoy him, so what I did instead was to take him with me to the markets and stand him a good dinner in their canteens. I also made sure that his fireplace never ran short of logs.

Although I might have forgotten to mention it, for many years now I have been spending my winters travelling about laying hedges on contract. When hedgelaying-time came round, Jim was always with me in the woods, trimming and bunching the stakes like there was no tomorrow, and I would never have dared to enter a hedgelaying contest without taking him along. Sadly Jim died ten years ago, and believe me he is still missed.

I suppose it's true to say that these days I am slowly winding down, although retirement is not a word I like or use. Some twenty years ago I bought fifty acres of grassland three miles from home, and ran a small herd of Charolais cattle, but now I have sold that land and have only the fifty acres my dad left me with. I go to market in the spring to buy cattle that I keep here and sell in the autumn. Sometimes I win and sometimes I don't, but I'm still a farmer and that's something.

Another thing I almost forgot to mention. My dad kept to the name of Lewis as his trading name, and it was 'Lewis' that the auctioneers always called out on his purchases. So although I have stuck to his Lichfield nick-name of Jake, to avoid confusion throughout this account, most people would have known him as Lewis or Shutkever.

He died in 1966 after a short illness, sixty-eight years of age and still working. The auctioneers at all the markets he attended honoured him by calling for a minute's silence, which I found a very moving experience and for many years now I have taken over his role at the markets, striving always to keep his name and reputation intact.

I now look back on a working lifetime that has been anything but dull. I know that I have been extremely lucky, first to have a father like old Jake to show me the way, and then to have made that journey at a time when the opportunity was there for those prepared to fight for it. I wouldn't mind being young again, but certainly don't envy those who are. With all today's technological gimmickry they seem to have lost the knack of enjoying themselves. All the fun seems to have gone. I still go to cattle markets, both as buyer and seller, but when I think back to hatchet-faced Frank and all those clowns who used to assemble at Gloucester market every Saturday, today's forays are dull indeed.

I know I've left it a bit late, but I would like to leave this account by stating my definition of a farmer. He's a man who, whether owner or tenant, lives and works on the farm. If he's lucky, he has a wife to help and children to follow. I do not include the large estates run by bailiffs or managers, because they're a different ball game entirely. They are the chain stores of the countryside, whereas my farmers are the corner shop. More than that, my farmers *are* rural England – and should there ever come a time when, through inept government policy, short-term local planning, misguided do-gooders or whatever, their way of life becomes unsustainable, they will be badly missed.

Wythwood Farm – August 2005

First published in Great Britain by:

Elliott & Thompson Ltd
27 John Street
London WC1N 2BX

© Harry Shutkever 2006

The right of Harry Shutkever to be identified as the
author of this work has been asserted by him
in accordance with the Copyright Designs
and Patents Act 1988.

ISBN 1 904027 52 0 (10 digit)

ISBN 978 1 904027 52 2 (13 digit)

First edition

Book design by Brad Thompson

Printed and bound in England by Athenaeum Press